The author is a scientist by profession and not a theologian. He was born near the end of WWII in the Middle East in the town of Baretly in the heart of the historical Assyrian Empire. He is an Antiochian Syriac Catholic by family and church attendance but believes that all Christians follow Christ. Following his postgraduate studies in the West he studied the Bible and Christianity through his own personal expedition and endeavour without any theology. This is his second book about the Christian faith also by Austin Macauley Publishers.

To every Christian, marginalised, discriminated, persecuted, and martyred for their faith.

George Habash

MY CHRISTIANITY

AUSTIN MACAULEY PUBLISHERS™
LONDON • CAMBRIDGE • NEW YORK • SHARJAH

Copyright © George Habash 2023

The right of George Habash to be identified as author of this work has been asserted by the author in accordance with sections 77 and 78 of the Copyright, Designs and Patents Act 1988.

All rights reserved. No part of this publication may be reproduced, stored in a retrieval system, or transmitted in any form or by any means, electronic, mechanical, photocopying, recording, or otherwise, without the prior permission of the publishers.

Any person who commits any unauthorised act in relation to this publication may be liable to criminal prosecution and civil claims for damages.

A CIP catalogue record for this title is available from the British Library.

ISBN 9781398476912 (Paperback)
ISBN 9781398476929 (ePub e-book)

www.austinmacauley.com

First Published 2023
Austin Macauley Publishers Ltd®
1 Canada Square
Canary Wharf
London
E14 5AA

20230913

The author thanks his family, the extended family, friends, colleagues, acquaintances, pastors, preachers, sermonisers, evangelisers and Bible scholars for helping him to make this book possible.

> **"By the rivers of Babylon we sat and wept when we remembered Zion."**
> **Psalm 137:1 NIV**

Psalm 137:1 was not written for only the Jews who yearned and wept for Jerusalem or Zion. It was also written for all of us Christians east of the Mediterranean Sea. In both cases, it was a prophecy written a millennium before the time of Christian era and before the exile of the Jews. Before that even Isaiah told us that yearning was true.

The Jews went into exile and Diaspora in old times, but now is the turn of the Christians who left Zion/Jerusalem, Cedars, Maaloula, Hagia Sohpia, and modern-day Nineveh. Yes by the rivers of Babylon yeah we sat and wept when we remembered thee.

Deny Christ or kneel for the sword? We kneel for the sword.

To every Christian who said yes to Jesus with the sword above his head, and to every Christian whose blood was spluttered on church pews or on church walls, and to every Christian who was and is shackled for his faith in Jesus I present this book; it is for you.

Prologue

This is my second book by Austin Macauley Publishers following my first book titled *I am a Christian*.

In this second book it will be a panoramic one. First I will go through the Bible from beginning to end picking up the highs and pivotal parts of the Hebraic and the Christian faith and simplify the text in order to make the reader discern what he/she reads.

Then I will handpick in full or part relevant Christian issues/events from my desk diaries and personal notes-both of happy-clappy celebration of rejoice and sorrow of the Suffering Church and the persecuted Christian believers. All Biblical quotations throughout will be from New International Version (NIV).

God designs the universe
c. 4000 BC

Based on Genesis in NIV Bible:

God is a Trinity, Father (F), Son (S) and Holy Spirit (HS) or simply three-in-one. He is timeless in that he knows the past and the present and the future, unlike us humans who are restricted by space and time.

At first God by fiat created, designed and fine-tuned the universe (heavens and earth) then sending light that would make light and darkness distinguishable in the form of day and night and this was the day one of the creation, then evening came and morning followed.

The earth and its environment is still covered with waters, so God divides the waters with expanse (divider) in two, until sky appeared, and this was the day two of the creation, then evening came and morning followed.

On day three of the creation the expanse expands and allows the dry land to appear and the waters gathered into seas. The land produced every kind of vegetation; then evening came and morning followed.

On day four of the creation the sky is clear, sun, moon, and stars appear as though the earth began to sense orbiting creating day brightened by the sun, and night gleamed by the moon, then evening came and morning followed.

On day five of the creation living water creatures of all kinds and flying birds of all kinds appeared, then evening came and morning followed.

On day six of the creation God created land biodiversity of livestock and wild animals. Then he created Adam (the first man) 'in our image, in our likeness' (in F, S and HS characters). From Adam's ribs God created Eve (the first woman). Although Eve is not mentioned in day six of the creation but is implicitly understood so. Then evening came and morning followed.

Note on day 1-5 God says what he created was 'good' but on day 6 he says it was 'very good' and creativity of the creation increases incrementally from day 1 to day 6.

On day seven (Sabbath in Hebrew or Shabtho in Aramaic or Shabtha in Assyrian) God's work is complete. He rests on the seventh day and made it holy (not the previous days but only this day) and Genesis does not mention evening and morning after this day because the creation is complete.

Adam and Eve were given the stewardship to rule and subdue the earth and multiply (fill), but both had broken God's commandment of obeying (the first sin ever) and that sin became known as 'the original sin' in which every human being must pay for it by inheritance and must end up by physical death (the first death). Satan (the Adversary) caused the first sin and the plan that God blueprinted was sabotaged.

When Adam and Eve sinned and are out of the garden they could not go back to the garden and undo the sin because as Albert Einstein said God does not play dice, but someone has to reconcile us to God and from above and that is Jesus Christ. Satan still has power to divert and deceive but his power will be obliterated for good when Jesus returns for his millennium reign.

The birth of the Hebraic nation of Israel
c. 2000 BC

Based on Genesis and Exodus in NIV Bible:

Redemption of mankind begins in a 'rescue mission' when 'God came near', but the process is not long only but a very long one.

It started when God tells Abraham (original Abram) to leave Ur of the Chaldeans in lower Mesopotamia and move to the 'Promised Land'.

Ur is uninhabited place and may have faced natural disaster so Abraham and his clan trekked along the Euphrates River up to Haran in northwest upper Mesopotamia. Then to the land of Canaan then to Egypt then he settled in Hebron in Canaan.

God made a covenant with Abraham that he will give him the land from the Nile to the Euphrates to his offspring. Later in the vision of Isaiah comes the prophecy of Egypt, Israel and Assyria fusing together.

He and his wife Sarah (original Sarai) are childless but at old age Sarah gave birth to Isaac. Abraham also fathered a son Ishmael before Isaac with Hagar the maidservant.

Isaac marries Rebekah and the two had two boys Esau and Jacob. Jacob marries Leah and then Rachel. Jacob had 12 sons by two wives and two maidservants. They are Reuben, Simeon, Levi, Judah, Issachar, Zebulun, Joseph, Benjamin, Dan, Naphtali, Gad and Asher. Jacob became Israel and the twelve sons formed the Hebraic nation.

The name Hebrew in English comes from Biblical word Ibret and means the crosser of the Euphrates River a term used at the time to mean immigrants as distinguished from natives, 'Abram the Hebrew' (Genesis 14:13 means Abram the (Iber) as first appeared in the Bible). Abraham did not invade Canaan like Alexander the Great but he just migrated to it. It was a plan motivated by God.

The drama begins when Joseph son of Jacob son of Isaac son of Abraham was sold into slavery to Ishmaelite tribe by his brothers at the age of 17 and in a roller-coaster down and up life in Egypt he reached the apex of the Egyptian society under Pharaoh. He was reunited with his 11 brothers and his father in Egypt, making an extended family of 70 people retaining their Hebraic roots and traditions.

Now Israel (son of Isaac), his 12 sons and descendants are labelled the 'Chosen People' whereas the descendants of Esau and Ishmael are not. Because Isaac was the son of the promise, but Ishmael was the son of slavery.

After 430 years in Egypt, the Hebraic nation swelled in number, like ('as the stars in the sky and as the sand on the seashore').

In c.1500 BC one of those Hebraic people is Moses who will lead the Israeli people from land of slavery in Egypt to freedom in the 'Promised Land' on the soil of Canaan.

About 600,000 Hebraic able men and a total of two million individuals roam the Sinai desert for 40 years searching for the Promised Land, 'a land flowing with milk and honey' that was covenanted with Abraham by God. It was Joshua after the death of Moses who entered the Promised Land crossing the Jordan River from east to west.

Bearing in mind the Hebraic people were not the invading people nor the sweeping army but mere migrants and have to use wisdom in their move for the land of the promise. Most territories were hostile and unwelcoming but had to pass, conquer and settle which took them 40 years to reach the land promised to them by God.

The history of the Hebraic nation has not been a plain sailing, it was a roller-coaster ride and concoct of triumph and tragedy. In 722 BC, Assyrians deported the ten tribes of Israel forming the northern kingdom into Assyrian captivity, although some Biblical scholars doubt that, but it remains a fact. The remaining two tribes of Judah and Benjamin of the southern kingdom were attacked by the Babylonians in 587 BC and the elites were taken into Babylonian captivity by Nebuchadnezzar after seizing Jerusalem and destroying the Solomon Temple or the first Temple. In 175-134 BC, the Maccabees fought the Syria-based Greek kingdom and its occupying power and in 66-70 AD the Hebrews revolted against the Roman rule with catastrophic outcome that saw the destruction of the second Temple (Jesus' Temple) and the dispersion of the Hebraic people.

It was in these tragedies of successive exiles that the Hebraic people became known as Jews or Jewish. It is an identity rather than a religiosity.

During the reign of the Third Rich, the Jewry faced extermination at the hands of the Nazis (1939-1945) and some six million Jews were Shoah-ed simply because they were Jewish. Twenty-two years later Israel's neighbours wanted to dump the Jews into the Mediterranean Sea but they fought back the 'six-day war' that ended not with their survival but with triumph.

This topic is outside of the scope of this title but it sheds some painful history faced the Jewish people.

The Jewish faith is not a proselytising faith, it is inherited or absorbed and from around 15 million Jews worldwide most are in Israel with equal number in America and there are fragmented presence in some major Western countries, still more Jews in Diaspora than in Israel.

The first Christmas
Jesus comes down from heaven to earth
c. 1 BC to 1 AD
Manifestation of God's redemptive plan

God is a Trinity (F. S and HS) and Jesus comes down from heavens to earth (first Christmas) and His ministry, is as follows:

Mary (Miriam) is a descendant of King David (c. 1000 BC), through his son Nathan and is betrothed (pre-marriage stage) to Joseph, also a descendant of King David but through another son, Solomon. Both are from Nazareth in Galilee in upper Israel.

Angel Gabriel appeared to a Jewish teen Miriam (or Virgin Mary) and said to her 'Hail Mary, Full of Grace, the Lord is with thee. Blessed art thou among women, and blessed is the fruit of thy womb, Jesus…' (Prayer of the Catholic Church based on Luke 1:26-38.

At the time of Jesus' birth Joseph and Mary (natives of Nazareth) are in the countryside of Bethlehem in Judea not far from Jerusalem. After Jesus' birth he is presented in the Temple as the firstborn. Then Joseph and Mary move south to Egypt until the death of King Herod the Great. They return to Galilee.

The Gospels do not focus on Jesus' childhood or boyhood apart from presenting him in the Temple on day eight, and his flight as a baby with Mary and Joseph to Egypt and then when he was 12 visiting Jerusalem with his parents and being active in the Temple.

Jesus is now about 30 years and comes to John the Baptist his relative for Baptism of Water in River Jordan. Baptism triggers Jesus' ministry. Jesus of Nazareth or Nasrat (in west of Galilee) or Jesus Nazarine moves to Kfar Nakhum (Capernaum) on the northern shore of the Sea of Galilee. Here being the metropolis town, rather than Nasrat he begins his ministry.

To inaugurate the Kingdom of God, he handpicked his 12 inner-circle disciples using simple statement 'follow me', and mostly are working class or blue collar in background and for the next three and a half years, Jesus and his followers started preaching the Good News of the Kingdom of God and the Message of Repentance and Salvation through the Son of God. He healed the sick, fed the hungry and performed miracles. He spoke plainly and in parables to inculcate his followers and the crowds. In his first miracle he turned water to wine-the old covenant into new covenant and summed up his mission by telling them love the Lord thy God and love thy neighbour.

Jesus like no other religion founder, gave freely without return just have faith in him and you are exalted.

These are the punch-lines of his ministry:

take your matt and walk,
take your sight and see,
your ears open and hear
your tongue loose and speak
un-cleanness is wiped clean
un-wholeness gone and be whole
take your spirit back and rise.
and then, take your cross and follow me.

The time has come for Jesus and his disciples to enter Jerusalem, the hub of the establishment and the Jewish elite. The crowd receive him with olive branches and shouts of Hosannas (deliver us) Son of David and 'baruch haba B'shem Adonai – blessed is He who comes in the name of the Lord' (based in Luke 19:38).

It is Sunday 10 Nisan 3793 (29 March 33 AD) (some say 6 April 33 AD) and Jesus buzzes to the Temple turning the tables and driving the traders out of the Temple-this is a house of God he told them. The Pharisees and elders were unnerved.

It is Thursday 14 Nisan 3793 (2 April 33), the Pascal full moon, the feast of Passover (Pascha in Aramaic and Pesach in Hebrew Jesus and the twelve were in the upper room for Passover meal or 'Festival of Freedom' or 'Egyptian slavery is past'. At the meal Jesus held a loaf of bread (matza) and raised it, 'This is my body given for you', he told them. Then he held a cup of wine (third cup) and raised it, 'My blood, which is poured out for you' (based on Luke 22:19-20). Then he began washing his disciples' feet.

In the Passover meal, Jesus initiates the first Holy Communion and the first priestly New Testament sacrifice.

Jesus hinted at the Passover meal that he will be betrayed and handed over to the authorities, resurrect, ascend and come again see John 12.

It is a time of prayer and Jesus knew the hour is almost here, when Judas Iscariot his own disciple hands him over to the authorities by the historic kiss of betrayal. This is a repeated history when Joseph was betrayed by his brother Judah and sold to the Ishmaelites some 2000 years earlier.

Then Jesus is taken from one place to another, from one council to another and from Sanhedrin to Pilate the Roman governor of Judea, it resembled a 'kangaroo court'.

'Judas the traitor' came to his senses and euthanized himself, for he believed in Jesus the man, not like the other 11 faithful, who believed in him as Jesus the Messiah.

It is Friday 15 Nisan 3793 (3 April 33) and Pilate tells the crowd and the elite whether they want to release free Jesus ('Bar Abba') or Barabbas; the crowd shouts for Barabbas because Jesus stated he is the 'King of the Jews' and 'Son of God' Pilate with no options for him left hands Jesus in to be whipped, dressed mockingly and crowned with thorns.

He is given his own cross to carry (Jesus carrying his cross of execution) through the alleyways of Jerusalem towards Golgotha a cliffy stony lot outside Jerusalem. He is nailed to one cross with three nails from 3 in the afternoon. He said 'it is finished' and he gives up his spirit at 9 in the evening. It is finished means any man or woman in him and through him is simply 'saved'.

'Two revolutionaries' with crime of felony were nailed with him flanking Jesus. One on his right said yes to Jesus and the other on the left said no. This represents humanity; those who believe in Jesus and granted salvation and those who do not believe and are condemned for eternity.

There are three crosses on Calvary as paintings show one giant in the middle and two dwarfed on the right and left. Jesus is between the two to separate the one who says yes from the one who says no, the sheep from the goat, the righteous from the condemned.

Jesus' body is taken for burial with five wounds in his body by Joseph of Arimathea and Nicodemus both secret believers.

Then darkness and stillness covered the earth for full Saturday 16 Nisan 3793 (4 April 33).

It is Sunday 17 Nisan 3793 (5 April 33), the feast of the First Fruits, and early at dawn Mary of Magdala and other woman hurry to the tomb of Jesus. The stone is rolled and angel of God tells Mary 'He is not here; he has risen.' Jesus glanced at Mary and said, 'Mary.'

Mary with rejoice responded, 'Rabboni.'

Jesus rose from the dead not like any human rising from sleep but Jesus left the linen with the linen intact, in other words transformed and glorified.

Jesus appeared to his disciples several times during his 40 days after the Resurrection. On Thursday on 40th day he ascends into heaven. After another 10 days he sends the Holy Spirit on his disciples and the Church of Jesus Christ begins (16 tongues/languages were spoken) and is until now. Those 16 nations became the microcosm of this universal church rushed with 'fire and winds of the Holy Spirit' without boundaries or sans frontiers. Then in Antioch the whole body of Christ was unified in one word, Christian, up to this day.

We wait for his second coming and his reign and our destiny for eternity with him:

From those 11 faithful disciples I personally admire most Saint Peter and Saint Thomas, the one who distanced himself from Christ thrice due to the political correctness of the time, and the one who wanted visual aids for the holes in his hands, feet and side before he believes. The first one said to Jesus during his Ministry, 'You are the Messiah, the Son of the living God' (Matthew 16:16; 10 words) and the second after the Resurrection said to Jesus, 'My Lord and My God' (John 20:28; 5 words). These two quotations from two disciples summarise the Christian faith that Jesus is the Messiah, Lord, Son in a triune God.

Jesus' mission is perfect and complete by becoming sin for us and dying for us. We in him only are reconciled to God and our salvation is granted in eternity with him. Any 'Christian is another Christ' or Christ-like.

The conclusion of the Christian faith is two days, Crucifixion Friday and Resurrection Sunday. On Friday our sins are nailed with Jesus to the cross, your past is dead and buried with Jesus. On Sunday we are made a new man-another Christ and saved forever; your eternity with Jesus is sealed as co-heir. The Friday's cross, the old rugged cross, is still there for anyone but is empty now, Jesus finished the work and with Jesus and in Jesus we conquer death.

On daily basis billions and billions the world over are invoking the name of Jesus in acts of prayer, adoration, supplication and fellowship something has no equivalent ever.

Jesus and John and the Book of Revelation
30-96 AD

The Book of Revelation is the last book of the Bible and remembering that the Book of Genesis is the first book of the Bible. John is the disciple Jesus loved and is also called John 'the Revelator' because to him Jesus conveyed the last words of Him to the Church, the seven churches at the time, and the Churches of our time.

When Jesus was baptised by John the Baptist in River Jordan in c 30AD then afterwards he started his public ministry. Walking along the Sea of Galilee (Tiberian Sea) he saw two brothers, James and John fishing and told them 'follow me' and be 'fishers of men'. Instantly, they dumped their nets and followed Jesus.

It is believed among scholars that Jesus was older than his disciples and this meant that most disciples were under 20 years old apart from Peter who was married and possibly 20 to early 20s in age. All disciples walked with Jesus for nearly three years partaking in his ministry and preaching.

The fifteenth-century mural of the Last Supper masterpiece by Leonardo da Vinci, which is in Milan, da Vinci depicts John the apostle to the right of Jesus and Judas Iscariot with a raised finger to the left of Jesus. It represents John who walked with Jesus for three years or so and being with Jesus at the foot of the cross on Crucifixion Friday when Jesus told his mother Mary or Miriam, 'Dear woman, here is your son' and to John he said, 'Here is your mother' as in John 19:26. Judas also walked with Jesus for three years or so like John but lost it in the last three days. He did not reach the finishing line, but John did.

John also was with Peter when alerted by Mary Magdalene when they hurried to the see the empty tomb on that Sunday morning, the Resurrection Sunday.

John and Mary moved to Ephesus the centre of the Christian faith after the Resurrection and he pastor-ed the nascent church. The church in Ephesus was one of the main seven churches in west of Asia Minor and also the seven churches mentioned in the book of Revelation. They were all connected by highways. In fact, John was the principal of the all seven churches in west Asia Minor.

John was head of the church in Ephesus when Emperor Domitian who ruled from 81–96AD and john may have lived to the end of the first century. Polycarp was one of his disciples who became bishop of Smyrna. Also his disciple was Saint Ignatius of Antioch.

All disciples of Jesus were martyred for their faith but John was the last surviving apostle. He suffered torture and persecution and his brother James was murdered and martyred. John then was exiled to the Aegean island of Patmos and it was there that Jesus spoke directly to John and John documented it in the Book of Revelation, the last book of the Bible and the last book of the New Testament and the last encounter with Jesus.

In the Book of Revelation some 63–65 years after Jesus' Resurrection (possibly in 95 AD), Jesus tells John to tell the seven churches at the time and our churches now. He tells him about end time prophecy of rapture, tribulation, second coming, the millennium reign and eternal life in eternity. Jesus will come and knock on the door. He is the alpha and omega, the first and the last and the beginning and the end.

The difference between the first book of the Bible and the last book is that in the first book or Genesis *Paradise is lost* but in the last book or Revelation *Paradise is restored*. In eternity there is no time or clocks, no four-dimension, no evening and no morning as in Genesis but continuous existence we call eternity in the presence of God.

David Jeremiah the eloquent preacher of the gospel says deity conquered eternity and eternity conquered time. This means time is gone and we eternally will be with God. There will be 'three news', a new heaven, a new earth and a new Jerusalem. In the Book of Revelation 'heaven is revealed' and of course 'hell exposed'.

In summary, Revelation is the last words of Jesus before his second coming. Jesus who came as a lamb shall return as a lion of Judah.

In Revelation, God speaks to Jesus and Jesus to John and John to all churches not the seven churches only.

Five hundred years anniversary of the Reformation
31 October 1517–2017

On 31 October 1517 (500 years in 2017) a Catholic monk Martin Luther, aged only 32 years, 'nailed' his 95 theses to the door of All Saints' Church in Wittenberg Germany. In his 95 theses Martin Luther opposed Church's teaching most in matters of practise and tradition rather than doctrine and faith. He opposed Pope Leo X indulges to build the Church of Saint Peter in Rome. Those writings triggered the start of the Reformation movement.

In 1520 Pope Leo X gave Martin Luther 60 days notice to renounce his actions, but he did not heed and in the following year 1521 he was ex-communicated.

Martin Luther presented 'Biblical Fundamentalism' and in 1522 he translated the Bible from Greek to German (with others, the work was complete in 1534). William Tyndale in Germany and Miles Coverdale also translated the Bible into English (complete in 1535). Between 1529 and 1531, the Reformation movement was coined as 'Protestant'.

The Reformation was summarised in five points or 'Five Solas' using the Latin words:

'Sola scriptura=by Scripture alone
Sola fide=by faith alone
Sola gratia=by grace alone
Solo Christo=through Christ alone
Soli Deo Gloria=to the glory of God alone'

The Reformation movement moved to England when in 1527 the Pope refused Henry VIII King of England permission to divorce his wife Catherine of Aragon, but in 1533 the king married his second wife in secret Anne Boleyn. That year the King was ex-communicated by the Pope and in 1536 the Church of England was established with the King as the Supreme Head.

The Reformation movement spread causing the second schism in the Church after the first schism in 1054AD when Byzantine (Orthodox) Church centred in Constantinople was ex-communicated from the universal Church centred in Rome.

Why Schism from outside not reform from within? Schism has weakened the Church's authority in the past, once mighty but is now weakened more. In modern time the Church is battling a tsunami of militant and aggressive form of secular humanism clamouring for atheism, church and Christian persecution, mega mass migration, ethnic cleansing, abortion, euthanasia, 'redefined' marriage and relationship, 'gender identity', un-canonical family structure and man-made bioethics. And above all a diluted form of Christianity with a diluted gospel to appease the world is preached, through the 'prodigal church'.

Every Church adopts the five points above, so was it worth splitting the Church or simply reform the Church within?

In 1965, the Catholic Church and the Greek Orthodox Church were reconciled. In the same way some Reformed Churches like the Lutherans and Anglicans, to mention a few, made similar approaches with the Catholic Church.

Martin Luther was not the first reformer. John Wycliffe died 1384 and John Huss 1372–1415 for example preceded him and what Martin Luther did was split the church for reform, but he did create a revival-ed church.

Later the Reformation movement was not monopolised by Martin Luther alone but entwined with John Calvin and Ulrich Zwingli where the three were coined as fathers of the Reformation. Then we have to wait for another long time until the advent of John and Charles Wesley to usher the Methodist movement and the Christian revival.

The rebirth of the State of Israel
14–15 May 1948

It is Friday sunset 14 May and up to Saturday sunset 15 May 1948 when David Ben-Gurion declared the rebirth and founding of the State of Israel (Hamadinat Israel).

Theodor Herzl, is a Jewish journalist from Vienna who attended the trial of French Jewish Army Captain Alfred Dreyfus in 1894 falsely accused of treason and imprisoned. He witnessed firsthand the abuse and humiliation he faced during his trial because he was Jewish and used as a scapegoat. He was later acquitted.

Less than three years later, The First Zionist Congress was held in Basel in 1897 a three-day congress from 29–31 August attended by 208 delegates organised by Theodor Herzl, the 'Visionary Zionist'. The congress concluded on a plan for the establishing of a homeland for the Jews in current Palestine.

After the congress in September he stated, 'At Basel I founded the Jewish State. If I said this out loud today, I would be greeted by universal laughter. In five years perhaps, and certainly in fifty years, everyone will perceive it.' Alas, a prophecy fulfilled in 1948.

According to Rabbi Jonathan Cahn, a Messianic Jew, Theodor Hrezl before he died in 1904 had a vision of the Messiah invoking him to prepare for his return.

On 2 November 1917 Lord Arthur James Balfour a Scottish and Foreign Secretary in the government of David Lloyd George, a Welsh and Prime Minister at the time of the British Empire issued the famous declaration known as 'The Balfour Declaration', a concise 67-word statement. It plainly says in it 'the establishment in Palestine of a national home for the Jewish people'. This statement in a letter was addressed to Lord Lionel Walter Rothschild the 'de facto' Jewish leader in England.

The Foreign Secretary signed the declaration and a month later on 11 December General Edmund Allenby entered Jerusalem through Jaffa Gate on foot in modest form to that mighty Jesus' entry on Palm Sunday.

The Turks left their posts and Jerusalem was back in the hands of the old Crusaders, some 400 years in the coming. That Balfour Declaration gave hope to the Jewish Diaspora to start packing for return to ancestral Ertz Israel and the toast 'next year in Jerusalem' became true.

In 1921 Warren G. Harding the US twenty-ninth President endorsed the 1917 Balfour Declaration in support of the Jewish people.

The Great War or WWI in 1914–1918 saw the Middle East partitioned between Imperial France and Imperial Britain, with Palestine coming under the British influence and later under the British Mandate and this was cemented by the League of Nations (precursor of UN) in 1922 specifically designating the land east of the Mediterrean Sea to the Jewish homeland and the land west of Jordan River for Arabs which became formal in 1947. On 14/15 May 1948 Israel declared its independence, but the Arabs attacked the following day. After the hostilities ended the UN recognised Israel as an independent state in 1949 and the first to recognise the new state was Harry Truman within 11 minutes and the second Joseph Stalin while Clement Attlee abstained. Harry Truman later boasted for his action saying, 'I am Cyrus, I am Cyrus' memorising King Cyrus who befriended the exiled Jewish people. Thirty-three countries voted for Israel's recognition (mostly Europeans and Latin Americans), thirteen opposed and ten abstained. At the time UN general Assembly was small.

The land east of Mediterranean Sea is now three parts, Israel, Gaza under Egypt and Judea and Samaria (West Bank) under Jordan.

Israel is surrounded by hostile Arab neighbours from north, south and east, but to the west is the Mediterranean Sea. The prevalent cliché in the Arabs mentality from 1948 is to 'drive the Jews into the sea'.

To protect its sovereignty from war mongering neighbours, Israel attacked its neighbours on 5 June 1967 and the war lasted until 10 June, and that is codenamed 'Six-Day War' for lasting only 6 days. The outcome was an Israeli over-victory capturing the Sinai Peninsula from Egypt and the West Bank (Judea and Samaria) from Jordan and the Golan Heights (Biblical Bashan) from Syria. And Jerusalem divided east and west before the War was finally and fully liberated on the third day and in Jewish hands when the Israeli Defence Forces smashed the Lion's Gate into the innermost east. The size of territorial Israel tripled.

The Arabs did blame the United States under Lyndon Johnson, but more blame was directed at the Soviet Union under Leonid Brezhnev for not fighting their war

On 6 October 1973 (10 Tishri) is Yom Kippur Day a big Jewish feast and after years of preparation Egypt and Syria attacked Israel from south and north, a copycat from Cyrus the Great attacking Babylon while the Babylonians were feasting. Their enemy gained ground in the first stage of the war with heavy loses but later and before the ceasefire on 26 October Israeli forces advanced on Golan Heights with views of Damascus from their binoculars and in the south they crossed into west bank of the Suez Canal.

The two wars in 1967 and 1973 saw the Arabs defeated in the first but with raised morals in the second for early gains and now the Arabs are ready for a negotiated settlement.

In 1978, Israel signed a peace treaty with Egypt at Camp David and later Jordon also signed a peace treaty with Israel in Eilat in 1994, but an agreement for a 'two-state' resolution known as Oslo Accords that was reached between the Israelis and Palestinians brokered by Americans in 1993 but was not implemented. Syria tried to reach a deal with Israel but an agreement failed to materialise up to this day.

Since then Israel fought many wars with its enemies but in smaller scales. Israel now is an advanced nation and one of world's major military powers but wants peace with all its neighbours.

On 26 July 2018, the Israeli Knesset passed a bill that 'Israel is the Nation-State of the Jewish people.' Also incorporated in the bill was that menorah is the emblem of the state, and Jerusalem is the capital of the state.

Moshe Dayan the hero of 1967 war told reporters while he was helicopter-ed from one battle front to another, one day we will live in peace with our Arab neighbours. A preacher on a Christian TV channel once stated that the conflict between Israel and its neighbours is humanly unsolvable, but will be solved by divine intervention-when Jesus descends for the second time. Israel, a miniature state in 1949 with under a million Jews is now a modern, thriving and powerful nation inhabiting 7 million Jews and all this is due to perseverance, sacrifices and determination of its people and here the quote from Benjamin Netanyahu, the current Premier of the State of Israel; 'Our policy is very simple. The Jewish state was set up to defend Jewish lives, and we always reserve the right to defend ourselves.'

The blow of the Shofar (Trumpet) from the Capitol Hill
20 January 2017

The Republican National Convention was held in Cleveland. Ohio on 18 July 2016 and on the second day Donald J. Trump was officially nominated to run for the Republican Party. On the fourth day, he gave his acceptance speech.

Donald John Trump was elected the 45th President of the United States of America on 8 November 2016 with his running mate Mike Richard Pence as his Vice President. Remember America today is described as the 'world's premier power.'

In the morning of Friday 20 January 2017 the President elect, his Vice President, the officials and guests gathered outside the Capitol Hill for the inauguration ceremony. It was George Washington, the first President who started the tradition of swearing-in ceremony in 1789, when he bowed and kissed the Holy Bible out of reverence.

The ceremony begins at 11:33 by the chairman of the Inaugural Committee followed by prayers of the following notable Christians:

Archbishop Timothy Dolan

Pastor Samuel Rodriguez

Pastor Paula White-Cain (the first female ever to pray at inauguration).

Then at 11:55 Oath of Office for Vice President Mike Pence and at 12:00 Oath of Office for President Donald J. Trump.

At 12:01 Donald J. Trump is officially the 45th President, and from 12:02 to 12:18 Donald J. Trump gives his first speech with a total of 1,453 words.

The second prayer round continued by notables, a Jew and Christians:

Rabbi Marvin Hier

Revered Franklin Graham (son of Billy Graham)

Bishop Wayne T. Jackson

And the ceremony ended after singing the National Anthem at 12:28.

The inauguration ceremony with six Judeo-Christian leaders is the biggest inauguration in US history. Franklin Graham told the gathering, 'There is one God and one mediator between God and mankind, the man Christ Jesus.'

All presidents except two used the Bible in the inauguration ceremony. Donald J. Trump used two Bibles, Abraham Lincoln's 1861 Bible and his own RSV Bible given to him as present by his mother in 1955 and he prided that 'his favourite book in the world'. His nationalistic views grew with him in 1980s when he was in his 30s seeing America humiliated by Iran holding American diplomats hostage and shortage of fuels at gas stations. This hit him hard and at the time of campaigning for election raised the bar with his chosen slogan to 'Make America Great Again' a phrase used by late President Ronald Reagan.

The title of this chapter was revealed to me by Bishop and Rabbi Jonathan Cahn, a Messianic Jew who revealed that the name 'Trump' is Biblical 'Trumpet' and related to the blow of the Shofar. He means that this is not accidental but God's appointed time for repentance and change of direction ushered by Donald J. Trump.

Donald J. Trump may be the richest President residing in the White House, but has a heart for conservative Christian values domestically and the world over.

On 15 February 2017 Donald J. Trump received Israel's Prime Minister and his wife Sara, the first of his meetings after the inauguration and in 25 minutes press conference both declared that peace between Israel and neighbours is based on (a) recognition of Israel as the State for the Jewish people (b) the security of Israel west of the Jordan-not hostile to Israel.

Later at Q&A session the first question was from David Prody for the Christian Broadcasting Network, a departure from past system dominated by others like CNN, NBC, BBC etc.

On 22 May 2017, Donald J. Trump flew directly from Riyadh to Tel Aviv (the first flight ever), then by helicopter to Jerusalem, the Capital of the State of Israel. He visited the Church of the Holy Sepulchre (the site of Jesus' crucifixion, burial and resurrection), the first incumbent president to do so and the Western Wall with a kippah on his head, also the first incumbent president to do so.

The following day he flew to Rome to meet Pope Francis, head of the Catholic Church.

On 6 December 2017, Donald J. Trump recognised Jerusalem as the Capital of the State of Israel (before his one year in office). He broadcasted live from the White House at 8 PM Israel time the following: 'I have determined that it is time to officially recognize Jerusalem as the Capital of Israel. While previous Presidents have made this a major campaign promise, they failed to deliver. Today I am delivering it.' The law was passed by the Congress in 1995 and voted by the Senate, but never implemented since then.

Although the UN General Assembly voted overwhelmingly (non-binding) against the move on 21 December, the President remains determined to implement the recognition and move the American Embassy from Tel Aviv to Jerusalem. After the vote Israel's Prime Minister stated, 'Jerusalem was, always will be Israel's Capital.'

In his speech at UN General Assembly in September 2019, the President stated that 'the future does not belong to the globalists. The future belongs to the patriots.' He meant no to man's government but yes to God's kingdom, as the Church teaches.

He also hosted a meeting at the UN regarding religious freedom around the world, the first President to do so and said, 'As President, protecting religious freedom is one of my highest priorities and always has been.' Religious persecution covers all religions, but his mind is with the suffering Church and the persecuted Christians worldwide.

On 1 December 2017 Mike Pence Vice President appeared on Christian Broadcasting Network with anchor David Brody talking about the issue of persecuted Christians and religious minorities across the wider Arab world.

Secretary of State George Pompeo met Pope Francis in the Vatican on 3 October 2019 on the issue of Christian persecution in the Middle East and promotion of religious freedom.

On 14 May 2018 and to coincide with Israel seventy-year anniversary celebration of the re-birth of the State of Israel, the American Embassy was moved from Tel Aviv and opened a new one in Jerusalem the capital of State of Israel-the first foreign embassy ever to open in Jerusalem. The President was represented by his daughter and her husband among other officials

Donald Trump contributed to the opening ceremony with a recorded message as were representatives of the evangelical churches and Jewish leaders. The city of Jerusalem is now defined as 'eternal and undivided city' for the first time since its inception by King David 3000 years ago.

On 21 March 2019 President Donald Trump said that he will recognise Israel's sovereignty over the strategic Golan

Heights that Israel captured in 1967 from Syria, that was annexed by Israel in 1981.

Four days later on 25 March he signed the decree recognising Israel's sovereignty over the Golan Heights in the presence of Benjamin Netanyahu the Israeli Premier.

The final note is that Donald Trump is a 'born again Christian' and that about 82% of Evangelical Christians voted for him.

On Friday 24 January 2020 Donald Trump is the first American President to join the annual 47th March for Life in Washing DC. He addressed thousands of Pro Life (anti-abortion) activists saying 'unborn children have never had a stronger defender in the White House'

On 26 February 2020 is the church designated Ash Wednesday and the White House in Washington issued the following statement:

'Melania and I wish everyone observing Ash Wednesday a peaceful and prayerful day. For Catholics and many other Christians, Ash Wednesday marks the beginning of the Lenten season that concludes with the joyful celebration of Easter Sunday.

Today millions of Christians will be marked on their foreheads with the sign of the cross. The imposition of ashes is an invitation to spend time during Lent fasting, praying, and engaging in acts of charity. This powerful and sacred tradition reminds us of our shared mortality, Christ's saving love, and the need to repent and accept the Gospel more fully.

We join in prayer with everyone observing this holy day and wish you a prayerful Lenten journey. May you grow closer to God in your faith during this blessed season.' Hallelujah.

The suffering church
The marginalisation, discrimination and persecution of Christians worldwide
'Faith under fire'
'Faith under rubble'

'Say nothing, do nothing'

2021 AD

The suffering church is the church that is marginalised, discriminated and persecuted in any form.

There is a consensus among the Western media and governments on the matter of Christian persecution to 'say nothing, do nothing' which also goes with the parallel norm 'don't ask, don't tell' because the fear of saying, doing, asking and telling is dangerous for the entities who are only concerned with globalisation or trans-national world that would brim their coffers.

King of Kings Jesus Christ on Good Friday was sentenced to die by Pontus Pilate, the Roman governor of Judea by obeying the demands of the mobs and the Jewish elite. This reminds me of a Good Friday's sermon given by a priest in the Middle East in 1960s who started his sermon by saying, 'God is sentenced to death'. In the Middle East's Christianity Good Friday is the highest day in the Church's calendar and the service starts from mid-afternoon and goes until sunset with churches full and attendance to capacity.

The persecution of Christianity and Christians started first with Jesus Christ, 'the author and perfecter of our faith'

(Hebrews 12:2). He was crucified for being the Son of God and King of the Jews.

Saint Stephen of the early Church was dragged and stoned to death in 36AD for being follower of Jesus Christ. This was the first Christian martyr ever.

From the original twelve disciples of Jesus ten were martyred, one survived and exiled to the Patmos Island and one hanged himself for guilt of retreating from Jesus' ministry.

From the first century to the current century, Christians, when time darkens, were used as fodder for the canons of their enemies who hated them for their faith. Pagan Romans, Persians, Arabs, Turks, Chinese and Japanese, Marxists and others did their utmost to strike a blow to the peaceful faith.

We are still in the first fifth of the twenty-first century and the Church worldwide is still being sacrificed. In the twentieth century it is documented that the Church worldwide gave martyrs more than the martyrs of all the past centuries put together. Millions of Christians sacrificed for their faith.

In this chapter, I will pick some atrocities from my lifetime that I have witnessed from TV screens and national newspapers and on internet. That does not mean I am overlooking massacres against Christians in the past, for example the Christian genocide in Asia Minor in early twentieth century by Ottoman Turks and their collaborators when a third of the population who were Christians were exterminated, forced to flee or died from hunger and disease. The genocide is known and acknowledged as the 'Armenian Genocide', but all Christians suffered Pontian Greeks, Assyrians and other Aramaic groups and the figure could reach 3 million Christians lost their lives for being Christians.

In the Armenian tragedy, the nation that lost 2/3 of its people and 9/10 of its soil by other people in the neighbourhood for no reason other than 'animus to Armenians as people and Christianity as a religion'. This is known by Armenians as 'Medz Yeghern' or the Great Crime in English committed by the turbaned sultans and their advocates mainly in the years 1915–1923.

'Saffar Berlik' is a mixture of Turkish and Arabic for troubled journey in English which the persecuted Christians of Asia Minor trekked at the time of WWI in April 1915 which is dubbed the long march of death southwards to cleanse the land from Christianity.

Recently from 27 September and 10 November 2020 an alliance between two states and mercenaries armed to the teeth with modern weaponry attacked the Armenians in Artsakh for 45 days in a war named the six-week war and resulted in land grab and the death of 2000–3000 defending Armenians, while Russia, EU, NATO and the world next door. The outcome was death, destruction, loss of territory and the displacement of more than 100,000 people, a third of the population.

With the exponential rise of Christian persecution worldwide this led to the creation of Christian support organisations to help and care for the persecuted brothers and sisters in Christ and dedicated a day in November for the suffering Church. Lately, the Churches designated Red Wednesday in November, just day before Thanksgiving Day as a day of sympathy and empathy with the suffering Church where churches and other prominent buildings are floodlit with red light for all to see.

'Christians experience discrimination, harassment or violence for His sake.' One pamphlet read.

In Syria and Mesopotamia despite Christians making a minority group but were well established in the society and their number grew. This sent fear signals to radicals to strike Christianity before it becomes strong. The same thing happened in Indonesia when the lone dictator was gone and the country seems to disintegrate like the former Yugoslavia, multitude of non-Christians moved into Christian islands and areas to dilute the Christian demography with no opposition from the government once secular and unreligious.

In China under the Communist dogma regards Christianity as 'Western religion' alien to the Chinese culture of atheism and the growth of Christianity alerts the elite that the Communist Party cannot be dwarfed by Christianity. So they do everything they can from closing churches, demolishing churches, arresting pastors and worshippers and removing thousands of crosses from church buildings.

Concerned Christian groups use the term genocide as it applies to the definition adopted by the international law. It is as simple as that and as painful as that.

About 25% of Christians are left in Baghdad or in the whole country and some gloomy reports say 10% is left while in Syria 1/3 is left.

In October 2020, the Vatican nuncio to Damascus said that half of the Christians in Syria have left the country.

'Christianity remains the most persecuted religion in the world and in many places even attempts at genocide are witnessed,' as one report put it

When the Romans declared Christianity the religion of the empire, the church in the fourth century became diluted comparing with the enthusiasm of the early church. That dilution remained in the church to this day creating two types of Christianity, church going Christianity and Christ believing Christianity.

The Middle East generally is not environ-friendly to Christians but hostile and this cause unease among Christians who began leaving their homelands even in 1950s and 1960s but in a slow scale.

When the central government is not sympathetic to Christian or weak in asserting its authority anti Christian sentiment becomes rife without provocation.

In a West African country, mobs demonstrated against the government for political reasons and monopoly of power by the ruler but on their way they torched Christian churches despite Christians being a minority and neutral in the conflict.

On 16 April 2015 a refugee boat carrying African migrants from Libya to Italy, a tense atmosphere arose on the boat between Christians and non-Christians. Twelve Christians were thrown overboard and dumped in the Mediterranean Sea and more could have died if not the Christians tied themselves together to prevent dislodging them. Fifteen attackers from Ivory Coast, Senegal and Mali were arrested upon the arrival in Italy. The reason was that when the Christians prayed for safe sea journey, the other non-Christians were offended and decided to punish them.

The land between the Tigris River and its tributary Upper Zab River in northern Mesopotamia is home to the Christians of the early believers who are dominantly Assyrians or Aramaic-speaking people. There are many towns and villages and archaeological sites of the past Assyrian Empire across that land but their presence was a roller-coaster dependent on who was in power at the helm of central government.

Due to vacuum in central power and weakness of the authority of the state, rag-tag rabble militia with totting-guns on pick-up trucks rolled un-hindered from Mosul a town of 2 million people which was conquered on evening of 9 and 10 June 2014 then moved south and further south towards Baghdad to consolidate their gains.

Once in Mosul the religious militia gave the remaining Christians of Mosul 24-hours' notice to deny Christ, pay protection tax money, leave or die by the sword.

The fall of Mosul and later east of Mosul, where Christians lived for centuries was a conspiracy when an alliance of disaffected former regime loyalists, sympathisers and the disbanded structures of the old regime came together as swat force to defy the then feeble central government. False intelligence, disinformation, quisling and fifth column resulted in surrender, retreat and capitulation of the defending forces which fled handing the Christian hub to the enemy.

On 3 August 2014 they seized full control of Sinjar (Shingal) to the northwest a predominantly Yazidi town (ethno-religious group).

Then between 6–7 August 2014 moved eastwards capturing almost all the towns and villages. All people fled. There is about 13 Christian towns and villages east, northeast and southeast of Mosul all were seized with a population of more than 100,000 that time, a quarter of Christianity in that country.

The militias roamed those towns and villages and wreaked havoc demolishing and burning houses and churches and marked N (for Nazarene) on every property belonged to Christians, which they meant for confiscation.

Look the land of mighty Sargon, Sennacherib and Nebuchadnezzar overrun and pillaged by nomad bandits totting guns on pickup trucks.

'Liberation' of the area started from October 2016 to 28 November 2016 after the central authority gained enough power to eject the militias. The occupation lasted 2 years and 2 months and 12 days.

The outcome was tragic, many Christians emigrated and many are still internally displaced and those who returned are few. They lost faith in the system but not in Jesus Christ. This is not a local or a regional matter, it is an international betrayal and the world must have power to impose peace among nations and within nations.

Between 10 and 13 May 2017 and in Washington DC the Billy Graham Evangelistic Association organised a meeting under the title World Summit in Defence of Persecuted Christians.

Church leaders and advocates from 130 countries met to address the ongoing atrocities committed against Christ's followers around the globe.

In the world today it is estimated that 215 millions in 50 countries where it is more difficult to be a Christian.

The meeting began with an address by Franklin Graham (son of late evangelist Billy Graham), President and CEO of the Association. This is the first ever world summit in defence of persecuted Christians.

Mike Pence VP of the US addressed the meeting the second day remarking that Christians are now the most persecuted group. '...we stand with you', he remarked in his 20-minute speech.

Studies found that 80% of Christian persecution is committed by Arabs and their co-religious. The other 20% is committed by the other religions and Marxist groups.

Almost 2 million Christians were killed in the civil war between north and south Sudan prior to the split and independence of the south.

In January 2015 in Niger 45 churches were attacked for no reason other than hate for events in France not related to Christians.

More than 12,000 Christians were killed in the past five years in the troubled and ungovernable northern Nigeria by a combination of tribalism, banditry and religious bigotry.

A Christian source said around 1000 people including priests and church leaders were killed in a series of attacks in Ethiopia, among them 750 in a raid on the Orthodox church of Maryam Tsiyon (Mary Zion) in Aksum around Christmas 2020 and after.

The Middle East from the Mediterranean Sea up to the former Persian borders is the Cradle of the Christian faith. De-Christianisation of the Middle East means emptying it from its indigenous Christian population.

Two bishops of Aleppo were kidnapped during the Syrian civil war and their fate is not known-either murdered or still in captivity.

Many priests are killed worldwide especially Catholic priests, nuns and lay workers.

The civil war in Syria and near civil war in its eastern neighbour and the emptying of Asia Minor from its Christian population saw the Christian heartland depleted of its

Christian population. Do not forget the Lebanese civil war 1975–1990 and the conflict between Israel and its neighbours.

In every country where Christians are minority they are persecuted and overlooked and discriminated against and treated as second, third-class citizens or no citizens at all. Slogans roared in Syria among the rebels with shouts 'Christians to Beirut' and once in Beirut the slogan will change-to the Mediterranean Sea.

In 2017 report an estimated 40000 people from 110 nations travelled to join militant insurgency in the Middle East with the main contributing countries, Turkey, Tunisia and Saudi Arabia including a few thousands from Western countries.

In 2020, released data show some 50,000 from all over the world joined the insurgency in the hope of replacing the native Christians, seize their properties and own them as slaves (among them 5,000 from Europe). Just get airway ticket.

In an interview on TV a Syrian lady said in Arabic, 'They came from everywhere to kill the Syrian human being.' This never happened before in that the whole world comes to Syria to overthrow the president and his government which has been in power since 1970.

Christian towns have been halved even quartered due to emigration. Christians are leaving their 'Christian land' in droves and handing it on platter to two regional powers. Non-Christians are also migrating to the West which they see is liberal, secular and un-Christian, a double-edged sword.

One regional power now conquers the vast areas of the Middle East from Persia to Lebanon. It is the second invasion of Nader Shah (1736–1747) to finish the job Nader Shah failed to do, in conquering the Christian lands.

One author summarised his book in statements: 'Persecution of minorities in the middle east, Western indifference and complicity, and the looming end of Christianity in the Middle East.'

'We will not allow terrorists remnant of the sword in our country to continue their terrorist acts. Their number has become small but they are still here,' another regional leader stated at press conference on 4 May 2020

In spring 2020, a television series in Egypt titled *The end* or el Nihaye in Arabic was based on a fiction drama that in 2120 i.e. 100 years from now Jerusalem will be captured and liberated with whole of its surrounding and the Jews will be dispersed to the countries they came from. This antagonistic view is in violation of the good terms between Egypt and Israel following the peace treaty signed in 1979.

Popes like John Paul II and Francis are often criticised by some zealot Christians for inter-religious dialogue by the two popes, but the Catholic Church has no option but to make dialogue for the sake of its faithful in hostile societies.

Persecution of Christians is a 'firewall' response to the power of the gospel on one hand and the defence of the outdated and crumbling system on the other. The New Testament is new, not obsolete, Good News not bad news.

More or less one million Jews left the Middle East and North Africa in 1945–1970 to make the new nation of hope leaving everything behind due to reprisals. At the time this was a big number.

First World War ushered the start of the decline of the Western civilisation but slowly and the Second World War hastened that decline which became apparent in the last decades of 1960s–1990s.

The West once centre, motivator and influencer of world events reached its climax due to its empowerment of civility and the Christian faith, but the West came out of the two wars tired and exhausted. So it looked for an alternative and a scapegoat. Christianity was the latter and secular society was the former.

Those events brought a new notion in the West's mind which implied that the two wars the West fought with the outside and within itself may usher a new thinking about a West devoid of religious identity and would be heaven on earth and eventually a new notion of West un-Christianised in order to appeal to the rest of humanity. The West wants to write off or end the bashing rhetoric by others such as 'the Christian West'. The West gradually, but systematically encouraged secularism based on human interpretation rather than religious or Christian ethics.

In recent times the West invented Globalisation (transnationalism). They introduced Sunday trading to deplete church attendance. Sunday trading was introduced to enhance the economy and subvert the weekly day of rest. Instead of people going to churches they rush the tedious journey to supermarkets, DIY stores and car boot sales, regardless of the impact on society's health and well-being. Sunday or Sabbath used to be the day of rest and worship but now is like any other day, they abandoned Jesus Christ.

The West went so far that it does not distinguish between Christian and non-Christian when applying for refugee status, even openly and publicly denying entrance or acceptance to persecuted Christians in order not to offend a part of the world that may in turn affect the trading or cause adverse financial outcome. Minorities have more privileges and rights than the natives because of their weight on swinging the election results.

The once peaceful and tranquil Western society is ruined with decline in all standards, living, governance, media, ethics etc.

They created inflated security system and tools of repression with 'abuse of power' and violating human rights in the pretext of combating illusory terrorism. It is reported that the security manpower doubled if not trebled in recent times. Ordinary people are filmed, photographed and monitored all the time. Tools such as voice-recognition, face-recognition and other up-to-date IT advances and modern technology have become common place.

They created despots worldwide and buttress them. Once overthrown they side with the masses until the dust is settled then creating new despots.

Before 1973, oil crisis (that followed Middle East's war) the price of barrel of oil was around 3 dollars, the West tinkered and retreated allowing the price sometimes to notch up to 200 dollars, and by this they drained their treasury and filling the coffers of oil sheikhs who use the revenue for expansion. Ignore fossil fuel and the destruction of the environment.

Retreat from the Middle East which started from taking Westerners as hostages by proxies in Lebanon and eventually handing it on platter to regional powers and by this altering the geopolitical power of the region and de-stabilising the region which directly affects the West itself.

Militant secular humanism gritted its teeth on the Christian faith in the examples of removal of the Ten Commandments from public places and Bibles from libraries and attacks on Christian festive seasons like Christmas and Easter.

Pope Francis visiting a strong Catholic country was told by the head of government that his country and his government no longer want the dominance of the Catholic Church but will opt for other faiths and religions.

The outcome of this is a West devoid of identity, devoid of coherency and devoid of morality. Once the West was Christian and advanced and envy of the world now is sclerotic, dilapidated and falling apart. Before people were governed by Christian principles and the society flourished as one spin doctor remarked and put it 'we don't do God' anymore.

When the West is blamed the Western Church (section of it) is not immune. The Church is responsible too but there are two types of Churches in the West, a Church that has conquered the world and is Bible-based and Christ-centred and a Church that is conquered by the world. The first teaches that God created man in his image but the second emphasised that 'God is in the image of man'. Better put by a preacher 'You cannot alter the Kingdom of God to match your lifestyle. You can alter your lifestyle to match the Kingdom of God'. Another preacher added 'enemy-occupied territory'. One went further to define a specified church as a 'prodigal church' which is the church that left the church (gospel and Jesus) and aligned with the world to produce religious consumerism. A church that takes orders, not the church that issues orders.

The Church was Greek until the conversion of Constantine and he accepted and legalised the Church making it Latin in about 350 AD. In legalising the Church the mission of the church expanded unhindered by the authority. Later it became State's Church and the Church transformed from 'decentralised' to centralised Church. This sudden and massive growth has diluted the structure of the Church from once in line of the first Apostles to the current world-cum-church.

Once the West preached Jesus Christ to the third world, now the third world is preaching Jesus Christ to the West.

During WWI every soldier was given a Bible. When the settlers reached the New World they conquered in the name of Christ. Names of many states and towns represented the Christian faith like Trinidad (Trinity), El Salvador (The Saviour), San Salvador (Holy Saviour), Christchurch, Whitchurch, Sao Paulo and the most common name in Spanish world is Santa Cruz (Holy Cross). Even their national flags and emblems are emblazoned by Christian crosses. But now they do not do God.

On 29 April 1607, the forefathers who landed in Cape Henry in the New World proclaimed America's land for Jesus Christ.

In the 1960s and 1970s as I have witnessed foreign students studying in the West married Western women and went home and continued to celebrate Western seasons of Christmas, New Year and Easter. Now this has reversed. Now it is the Western man or woman who follows the other customs even when that required changing their religion and name.

In early 1990s a leader of a large Western political party said, 'I am "agnostic,"' which is a soft term for atheism. A Western President said before he died that when he dies God will say to him, 'Welcome home my agnostic son.' A Western politician derides the Cross in order to satisfy followers of other religion to gain electoral votes. Western royals plagued with high divorce rate once symbols of Christianity.

State-atheism once practised in Communist countries, now is flourishing in the West. The West has abandoned nationalism and forsook patriotism. The main parties centre, left and right have abandoned the nationalistic and patriotic agendas in order to win elections. This led to rise of European and Western far right parties or groups seeking the society be returned to the old Western-Christian culture, The far right is not anti-foreigners but anti-existing order of decline of the Western way of life.

In this culture and system of today you may attack Jesus and the Christian faith without a backlash but you cannot criticise another religion or its founder.

On 11/9 2001 the President said on TV that the religion of the attackers is 'Peaceful'.

On 7/7 2005 the Premier said on TV the same thing (copycat) that the religion of the attackers is 'Peaceful'. It is the practising Christian and the church goer who said that, not somebody from the religion of the attackers to say that their religion is peaceful.

In the 1950s and 1960s the politics in the West was pure centre or left or right, but now the boundaries are gone, a leftist can be a believer and a conservative unbeliever. A leftist can be both ethical and unethical and the conservative the same. Gone are the days when one represented the real politics. What matters is personal power and wealth, even if that requires abandoning the principles and culture. A socialist can be much wealthier than the conservative one. A

Christian politician has to comply with Party line even when in conflict with his faith.

A politician may make personal deal with a minority group in a 'multicultural' society in order to reach the high office even if that meant sidelining the native culture.

A Western preacher was taken to court by an immigrant from a minority group because he felt the preacher offended his religion. In another case a mayor decreed that Sunday sermons be submitted to the council to check the contents in case violating political correctness.

What the modern Western man is doing is the removal of the notion of sin which means that there is no longer right or wrong and that is leading humanity to self-destruction.

The Middle East is handed over to regional powers via secret deals and surrender pacts. Many oppressive and anti-Christianity regimes were brought to power by Western intelligence. Millions of Christians were killed and forced to leave their ancestral homelands without the West lifting a finger.

Western media, universities, education system are indoctrinated with political correctness and Christian persecution is given a green light by the West. They can stop it if they want, but they won't.

When Russia ended Communism, Communism did not end and Communistic atheism did not die it returned back to the West where it was invented. Marxism was invented by the West not agrarian Russia, Iben Thranholm said in an interview.

It is a war on Christianity because Christianity says no to abortion, euthanasia, suicide, divorce, alcoholism, narcotics, social injustice and mal-governance. This does not fit with the

West today. Iben Thranhom went further, 'the West has become Satanic-demonic.'

The archbishop of the Syriac Orthodox Church in London Athanasius Toma Dawod invited three Middle Eastern bishops to attend the opening and consecration of the first Syriac Orthodox Cathedral of Saint Thomas in London on 24 November 2016. The three bishops were Nicodemus Daoud Sharaf of Mosul, Timothius Mousa Shamani of Saint Matthew's Monastery near Mosul and Selwanos Boutros Alnemeh of Homs and Hamath. Their visa application was rejected by the UK and the case was widely reported in the media including The Catholic Herald, The Times and a Christian magazine. Three men of the cloth refused entry would have not altered the statistical net migration.

The consecration of the Cathedral was presided by Patriarch Ignatius Aphrem II the head of the Syriac Orthodox Church of Antioch who resides in Damascus.

The official respond, was that the bishops lacked funds, and that they might not return to their countries. This is an absurd response for three bishops who stood with their dioceses at the heights of Christian cleansing from their cradle. This is a moral persecution and no different than physical Christian persecution.

In May and June (only) 2020 as reported by the media 1443 willy-nilly migrants on boats landed on the UK shores from France, but three pious bishops were refused entry visas.

Due to decades of Middle Eastern Christian persecution from 1970s onwards, now the cradle of Christianity is depleted from its Christian population. There are now large communities of these Christians in the US, Canada, Australia, New Zealand, France, Germany and Sweden. Even in other smaller Western countries, but they are shunned in the UK because they do not do God. These Christians have become like the Hebrews and Armenians 'stateless diasporic people'.

'The Christians who decided to remain are a small minority that continues to become smaller', one writer observed.

The West in recent times does not approve or disapprove the Christian persecution but it does allow it to happen. And is able to raise a finger if it wanted and in terms of colours it goes for Amber, not green or red.

The Holy Land is Judeo-Christian. Outside Israel proper I mean in Judea and Samaria (4 million) and Gaza (2 million), 6 million population in total there are only 47000 Christians left. Bethlehem the birth town of Jesus is only 25% Christian, once was 84% a century ago.

Until 1500 AD, Christians constituted half of the population of Asia Minor (called also the 'other Holy Land') and in 1914 was third of the population, but now only 2 per 1000 or 2000 per a million of the population. Where are those Christians and where are their hundreds of hundreds of churches?

Lebanon is a tiny country in the Levant just above Israel but much smaller and since its independence from France in 1946 it adopted a system of confessionalism in governance where the power is distributed along the ethnic-religious components. Christians fared well but in an unease climate and the country blossomed and became heaven on earth more popular than the European resorts.

In 1975, while Christians were leaving a church they were machine-gunned by assailants and that triggered the Lebanese civil war from 1975 to 1990.

In the civil war every ethnic and religious group fought for survival but by the end of the civil war in 1990 the country was shattered and the outcome was a Lebanon that no longer was heaven on earth. Christians lost ground and many emigrated.

The system is still the same but with clipped wings for Christians and during the civil war many Western hostages were taken by proxies of the regional power that brought humiliation to the subjected Western governments with their backs against the wall. They fought WWI and WWII but cannot rescue their citizens.

The West describes itself as a democracy but this is an obsolete definition which is no longer applicable. Democracy and freedom went and go together but freedom does not exist in the West anymore. The Western system has become a flawed and frayed system. What the West means by democracy is ballot papers, and the counting nothing more nothing less but everyone wants to win by whatever mean. Take for example a regional country which votes for three parliaments (regional, national, EU) creating three bureaucratic and dysfunctional bodies in the name of democracy which does not exist. Ignore council elections.

What is the function of elections when the political party lines are broken in that the conservatives are not conservative and the socialists are no longer socialist and those betweens are no longer between? People who vote, vote only what their parents or grandparents voted with no regard for the candidate standing or belief. A conservative can be very liberal and a leftist can be very conservative. There is even a huge tendency for tactical vote, which means voting not for your candidate to win but vote for any to make the candidate you don't like lose. Politics is dead.

A leader of a political party once made a secret deal with a minority group that would swing the election results to his favour. He promised them once elected to give them a free reign to popularise their culture and religion. He won and stayed in office for 10 years or so and would have stayed more years if not replaced by his own party. Almost all the population he governed did not know about the deal.

Today no one can say for example I am a French nationalist or a German nationalist or any nationalist and if they say it meant for passport. Only the far-right advocates can say that but they are labelled as bigots by the mainstreams. Nationalism has melted in the crucible of globalisation (transnationalism) or borderless world.

A Premier in northern Europe once said we have no culture and meant his culture and in his mind multi-culture is better.

In 1831, a European Christian visited America and found that the church was powerful and the nation blessed. Despite separation of state and religion he found no separation between God and state.

In the 1980s Swiss youths rebelled against the state and when asked why? The answer was 'we do not exist' and 'we want to be'. A Christian at the time commented that the best fed people and the best clothed and the best quality of life in the world do not exist and want to exist.

Pope Benedict XVI says the West was a cultural achievement with history. Christianity gave Europe freedom, liberty, progress, family, society, health, education, hospitals, universities, science, culture, law and order. For example

Ireland before Saint Patrick was wild. Saint Patrick and his Christianity created Ireland which never existed before. The whole of Europe was fiefdoms and ganglands. EU gave Europe nothing but hollow colossal buildings, bureaucrats and influx of mass migration.

The pre-Napoleonic French Revolution of 1789, the Russian Revolution of 1917, the reign of Joseph Stalin and the rise of Adolf Hitler and his national socialism in 1933 altered the West's psyche. Moreover, Charles Darwin's on the origin of species, Karl Marx's Das Kapital, Sigmund Freud of psychoanalysis, WWI, WWII and Albert Einstein's relativism, made the West relativistic and caused the psyche of the West to be altered. Joseph Ratzinger described that as 'dictatorship of relativism'.

Bertrand Russell (1872–1970) may have liked Jesus a bit, but he puts Buddha ahead of Jesus. The Buddha's lands of China and the Far East are crumbling by the weight of the gospel of Jesus Christ despite severe persecution. Bertrand Russell is not alive today to see for himself. The gospel is making inroads in India as well. Up to 70 million Christians exist in China today mostly in unregistered House Churches. One million Chinese come to believe in Jesus Christ every year according to a Christian source.

Even the continent of Africa in 1900 records show only 9 million Christians (6–7%) and these mostly in Biblical Egypt, Sudan and Ethiopia but now half of Africa is Christian nearly 670 million Christians. Jesus Christ' gospel is spreading in Africa like a wild fire. Churches are building hospitals, schools, universities, health clinics, orphanages, and feeding centres. This is what John Paul II said in the 1990s that Africa is 'the new homeland for Christ.'

Eric Blair in his book nineteen eighty four published in 1949 under the pen name George Orwell imagined the world governed by 'thought police' dictatorship where every aspect of life is controlled even the power of personal thinking-police in the brain.

Fulton J. Sheen, a well-known American Catholic Bishop (1895–1979) said before people lifted placards and marched for the things they knew but now they march but they don't know why and what for. This was decades ago and he did not live longer to see the disaster today of the Western society.

The present West has created a society insipid and soulless. When people march, each person has one agenda different from the one in front or the one behind but all have one aim-rebellion.

The Bishop also point out that the West want Christ without the cross whereas Communism want the cross without Christ. Each picks what it suits.

Marx said, 'Religion is the opium of the people,' and Francis Crick a well-known scientist in the twentieth century used to tell his colleagues that 'Religion is error of past generations.' This is the exact meaning of Marx's, but in different words.

Friedrich Nietzsche said, 'God is dead,' but we Christians say Nietzsche is dead.

Decades ago I had a European friend at the university and I used to tell him that God created man but would reply that 'man created God'. He was another copy of Joseph Stalin, both former monks, both present atheists.

Joseph Stalin Bragged once at the helm of the Kremlin that he will show on television the last Christian and the last priest.

In 1966, Svetlana Alliluyeva (1926-2011) the only child and daughter of Joseph Stalin entered the American Embassy in Delhi, India and asked for asylum status and she was taken to Rome and then to Switzerland and from there to America the following year. She was baptised in the Orthodox Church in 1962 and in December 1982 she became Catholic.

After the dissolution of old system in 1989 she returned to Russia, then back again to America. She died happy embracing the Christian faith.

One secret of Fatima Portugal apparition in 1917 was that the Great War will end and Russia will return to the faith. This is exactly what happened, no longer Leningrad but Saint Petersburg.

A Christian preacher in the 1990s stood in front of Vladimir Lenin's mausoleum in Moscow and said, 'Lenin behind me is dead but Jesus is alive.' This is a triumph for theism and defeat for atheism.

In the Middle East the depletion of Jews after 1948, then Christians 1975–2020 and the buttressing of 'Butcher of Baghdad' 1968–2003, Butcher of Khartoum 1990–2019 and the new Sultanate in Constantinople since 2000. All hands in gloves with the Western axis despite militancy and bellicose approach by them.

Erwin Lutzer outlines economic decline, educational decline, moral decline, legalism to silence Christianity and putting other religions before Christianity as the doing of the West.

The West departed from flourished ethical Christian culture into unethical culture of broken society fragmented into fiefdoms of super rich, super poor, food banks, Sunday car boot sales, charity shops, homelessness, bankruptcy, bomb sites, terrorism scenes, and 'industry' of football, celebrities, showbiz and media.

In the 1950s preacher evangelist Billy Graham told a packed stadium in a Western city that you don't know where you have come from, you don't know why you are here and you don't know where you are going. If this message was meant for the status of the West in the twentieth century, it would almost certainly meant as a prophecy for the lost, insipid and spiritless West in the twenty-first century.

Examples of Christian Persecution Worldwide

Jesus was persecuted and Christians have been persecuted from the time of the early church. Christians are marginalised, discriminated and persecuted throughout the centuries up to this time. Christians continue to suffer for their faith day after day especially when Christians are minority. Even in the West Christians are marginalised.

Here are some examples that were largely picked and widely reported by the media and this does not mean other cases of Christian persecution are overlooked; Christians suffer every day and even every moment.

The kidnapping of one of Mosul's Bishops
2008

29 February 2008 is Friday and in Lent, and a Chaldean Church (which is Eastern Rite Uniate) in Mosul is packed with celebrants to commemorate Jesus' crucifixion which is annually celebrated and venerated in the Stations of the Cross services in the entire Catholic World during Lent and it is late in the afternoon when the service ended. The Bishop Palous Faraj Rahho {aged 65 and Bishop since 2001 and priest since

1965) was in his car when it was hit by bullets killing the driver and two bodyguards and in gun battle he was kidnapped at gunpoint and taken to unknown place and the kidnappers demanded a ransom of 3 million dollars for his release.

The Bishop with poor health and under heavy medication possibly died while in custody. He was buried secretly.

Two weeks later on 14 March 2008 his grave was located and exhumed for Christian burial. He was buried in the Christian town of Karemlash southeast of Mosul. His junior priest Fr. Ragheed Aziz Ganni and three deacons were murdered the year before.

Heroism of Aasia Bibi the Punjabi Christian
2009–2019

In 1983, I asked a Punjabi student studying for a Master's degree in this country if there are Christians in that part of the world. His answer was yes, but all are street sweepers.

About 10 years later I saw a picture of a Christian man holding a broom in a Christian magazine with the caption underneath saying the only job for this Christian man is street sweeping. All this is an institutionalised discrimination against the Christians by depriving them from education and forcing them to earn living as deprived poor labourers with few options left for them apart from sweeping, brick kiln labourers and farm or domestic slaves. But these brethrens are brave enough and to quote Karl Marx they have nothing to lose but only their chains. This reminds me also with the status of Jews in old Yemen, the poorest country in the world, where also Jews worked as street sweepers, but after 1948 they made Aleyah to Israel. Now they are building the modern State of

Israel. I hope one day a Yemeni Jew will become a Chief-of-Staff stated an Israeli general.

Aasia Bibi is married to Ashiq Masih and they have five children. They are Christians and Catholic by Church attendance. They are poor, the common status for Christians in that part of the world. She is from Sheikhupura in Punjab province.

In 2009, she was working in a farm with other women from different religion and a matter arose that the other women accused her of drinking water from the same cup because as 'unclean', Christian she should not do that. A quarrel erupted and words were exchanged which ended by accusing Aasia Bibi of blasphemy against the religion or prophet of the land and was arrested. This is a frequent occurrence to trap the poor Christians once disputes arise.

In 2010, she was sentenced to die for blasphemy despite pledging her innocence.

Shahbaz Bhatti, a native Roman Catholic Christian and minister for minorities and member of the ruling party at the time stood by her and others in similar cases and pledged 'I will die to defend their rights.' He was assassinated outside his parents' home on 2 March 2011; his car was hit by at least 10 bullets.

And in 2015 she appealed against her conviction. And on 31 October 2018 the Appeal Court overturned her blasphemy conviction.

Aasia Bibi was taken from prison to a secret safe location and under guard in order to facilitate her departure from her native country, without harm and join the rest of her family

While in prison she affirmed her belief in Jesus Christ, and refused to recant her faith or convert a condition that would set her free. She always protested that she was provoked into verbal exchange.

Upon her acquittal her husband appealed to US, UK and the West for safe haven for the persecuted family, Canada responded to the appeal, but the UK Premier rejected the appeal and ashamedly declared that Aasia Bibi will not be accepted in her country. This was according to a Christian magazine.

In matters of Christian persecution worldwide the Western media and governments adopt the policy of political correctness 'say nothing, do nothing'.

Aasia Bibi is now 51 was allowed freedom on 29 January 2019 and joined her family in Canada on 8 May 2019. Aasia Bibi endured 'hell' and the youngest two daughters were brought up without their mother. All this is for the sake of Christ and all this is for being Christian in faith. There are now 70 other cases of blasphemy against the Christians in that country and all face the possibility of capital punishment.

All Saints' Day in Baghdad
31 October 2010
'Martyr–Church'

In the West is pagan Halloween's Day (pagan means pre-Christian practice) but in the calendar of the Catholic Church is the eve of All Saints' Day and faithful are gathered for the Sunday Mass in the middle-class area of south of central Baghdad.

The Church of Our Lady of Deliverance (now elevated to Cathedral) is a beautiful Catholic Church high above the ground emblazoned by a huge, curved arch which holds a huge cross high in the air; it belongs to the Syriac Catholic Church of Antioch (originally founded by Saint Peter disciple of Jesus Christ) that was built in the 1950s.

It is early evening Mass or Service at 5 pm local time and the church pews are packed with faithful and the service is conducted by two young priests Father Thaer Saadalla Abdal 32 (ordained 2006) and Father Wassem Sabih Qas Boutros 27 (ordained 2007).

About six terrorists motivated by their religion storm the church after a car bomb that killed the guards outside the church. They stormed the church while the priest was reading from the Bible, they shot with automatic guns, threw grenades and with their bellies wrapped with suicide belts.

Followers of Jesus in the house of worship killed and maimed and their bodies and bloods scattered everywhere. The graphic picture is that about 120 worshippers, among them two priests and one deacon were in the church.

The massacre lasted from 5 to 9:30 pm when the ammunitions of the attackers depleted and ended at 10 pm.

Father Thaer Saadalla Abdal was shot while kneeling. His brother was also shot.

Father Wassem with a cross in his hands pleaded with terrorists not to harm parishioners but was pushed to the floor and shot.

The church now full of fallen bodies and those injured about fifty hid in the sacristy and twenty hid in the baptistery. This group of 70 represents the injured and the survivors.

One family lost four members, two families each lost three members and five families each lost two members. Among the total lives lost one unborn baby and a toddler of 3 years with the name Adam who was shot between his eyes while in the hands of his mother to inflict suffering on his mother.

Almost all martyr and survivor worshippers are not native Baghdadis but natives of Nineveh Province in the north of the country specifically in metropolis Mosul and the surrounding Christian towns.

What happened in that early evening Mass was not only a terrorist act on peaceful Christian worshippers but a cold-blood and pre-meditated horrific massacre.

The Vatican is studying the case of the 48 martyrs (men, women and children) for later beatification but this is a slow and long process. This ordeal of five-hour bloodshed and massacre in a service of sacrifice of the bread and wine has become a true body and blood sacrifice in the example of saint Oscar Romero of El Salvador who was shot dead while preaching on Good Friday in the 1980s. In his March 2021 visit to that land Pope Francis called the Church in that country of Mesopotamia a 'martyr-Church'.

The disappearance of two Bishops in Syria
22 April 2013

On 22 April 2013 the Greek Orthodox Bishop of Aleppo Poulos Yazichi and the Syriac Orthodox bishop of Aleppo Youhana Ibrahim, suddenly disappeared.

And since then despite many efforts being made by the church and activists locally, nationally and internationally, nothing was obtained about their fate and whether they are alive, taken against their will or killed for their faith. Add to this no claim of responsibility was made by any group or the demand for ransom for their freedom. There is ample of conspiracy theories for their disappearance.

The massacre on the Libyan Mediterranean seashore
15 February 2015

A shocking video was released by fanatical militia influenced by their religion which showed 21 Christians dressed in red/orange colour jumpsuits and readying them up for beheading because of their faith in Jesus Christ.

Twenty were Egyptian Copts and one Ghanaian, all working in Libya as migrant workers. They were rounded up in the coastal town of Sirte in December 2014 and January 2015. These men were picked up among other workers using their Christian names as proof of their Christianity.

Each of the 21 Christians remained faithful and said, 'Jesus, help me.' They were beheaded following the verdict of the executioners: 'The people of the cross, followers of the hostile Egyptian church.' The bodies of those Christian martyrs were repatriated home.

On Christmas Day 2019 and in a copycat for this bloodshed 11 Christian men were abducted from Nigerian Borno State and beheaded in the same pattern. They dressed their victims in red/orange colour jumpsuits and kneeling and above each stood a knifeman, according to a Christian source.

The Massacre of Easter Sunday in Sri Lanka
21 April 2019

Sri Lanka (formerly Ceylon) is an island south of India and a holiday destination for many Westerners. In the east coast is the town of Batticaloa and on west coast is the town of Negombo and beneath is the capital Colombo. Christians constitute 7.6% in a population of 21 millions.

It is Easter Sunday in the West and Resurrection Sunday elsewhere and all churches are packed worldwide and between 8.30–9.00 am local time three churches and three hotels are bombed by nine body suicide bombers – eight blasts in total.

In Saint Anthony's Shrine 160 worshipers were killed or injured. 'It was a river of blood,' quoted one eyewitness.

In the Catholic Church of Saint Sebastian in Negombo packed with 1200 people 62 worshipers were killed. In Zion Church in Batticalao 30 worshipers were killed.

In total, more than 300 died from the blasts and more than 500 were injured from all blasts. More explosives were seized by the authority that was intended for further attacks.

Following Easter Sunday bombings all churches were closed until 12 May 2019 when masses and services resumed but under heavy security measures.

On Twitter, a furore erupted debating two tweets by two former US politicians who under-toned the word Christians to 'Easter worshippers' to avoid offending non-Christians and also to avoid saying Christians were the target of violence.

Former US President and former US Secretary of State tweeted respectively:

'The attacks on tourists and Easter worshippers in Sri Lanka are an attack on humanity. On a day devoted to love, redemption, and renewal, we pray for victims and stand with the people of Sri Lanka', Barack Obama 21 April 2019, 7:02 pm.

'On this holy weekend for many faiths, we must stand united against hatred and violence. I'm praying for everyone affected by today's horrific attacks on Easter worshippers and travellers in Sri Lanka.' Hillary Clinton 21 April 2019, 6:17 pm.

Christians cum Christianity

I have selected five biographies and three topics that are of interest to average Christian faithful.

Martin Luther King, Jr.
1960s

As a boy growing under segregation in America Martin Luther King noticed the injustice of humanity to humanity. Once sitting next to his father who was driving a car he was stopped by the police and the police shouted at him you boy, but his father was angered and said I am no boy this is a boy pointing to his son Martin.

Martin was born on 15 January 1929 and in 1955 Rosa Parks in segregated America was arrested in Alabama for not giving her seat to another person on a segregated bus. That incident blew out of proportion and ushered in the Civil Rights Movement in the United States and continued until late 1960s.

His father was active in the movement and later the son also joined and became the leader of the movement until his assassination in Memphis in 1968.

Martin Luther King, a Baptist preacher and a gifted sermoniser became the prominent figure of the movement, leading marches and giving speeches demanding equal rights for all Americans.

The name Martin Luther was chosen for the namesake of the German monk who led the Reformation movement out of the Catholic Church.

Both father and son were Baptist ministers. They adopted civil disobedience and peaceful protest to expose the hated racial injustices and demand equality through law on one hand and Bible on the other.

In November 1963, John Fitzgerald Kennedy the first Catholic President of the United States was assassinated in Dallas, Texas while his wife sitting next to him in a moving limousine. The news reached Martin Luther King, and stated that this thing will happen to him too. Less than five years later in 1968 he was shot dead, a prophecy he foretold.

In the early 1980s, I visited a Catholic monastery in this country and saw on the wall a framed picture with extracts from Martin Luther speech arranged in poetry lines 'I have a Dream' statements from his speech 'March on Washington' in March 1963 as he stood on the steps of Abraham Lincoln Memorial, the sixteenth president.

Later following that march on Washington, he was awarded the secular Nobel Peace Prize in 1964.

15 January every year is a public holiday in the US to honour the Civil Rights leader's memory. At the time of his death he was survived by his wife and two daughters who continued in his footsteps seeking equality and faithfulness to Jesus Christ.

Two Christians walk on the Moon
20 July 1969

This year (2019) comes the fiftieth anniversary of man's first landing on the Moon. All media, radios, televisions, newspapers and magazines celebrated the iconic occasion with ample coverage and the great work by NASA and the three heroic player astronauts Neil Armstrong, Edwin Aldrin (Buzz) and Michael Collins.

It started in Florida's Cape Canaveral on 16 July 1969 at 13:32 local time when Apollo 11 lifted off taking the three astronauts on their mission to conquer the Moon.

Neil Armstrong and Buzz were in the lunar module (Eagle) and Michael Collins in the command and service module orbiting some 70 miles above.

The lunar module landed on the Moon on 20 July at 102:45 with elapsed time of 89 hours and 13 minutes (subtract the two times).

Data from my notes say that 1 million people came to nearby area to watch the lift off live. It was about nine years earlier when President John Fitzgerald Kennedy stated that he will put a man on Moon before the end of the decade-a prophecy fulfilled.

On return to earth, the lunar module lifted off with the two astronauts from the Moon at 124:22 on 22 July to rejoin the command and service module and with the third astronaut (21 hours 37 minutes time on Moon).

The spacecraft headed to Earth splashing the Pacific Ocean on 24 July at 195:18:35 with total elapsed time of eight days.

About 350 kilograms of Moon's rock samples were brought to Earth for laboratory tests. Conversations from the Moon were heard like 'the first time humans walk on alien world' and 'that's one small step for man, one giant leap for mankind' are referred to Neil Armstrong the mission commander.

When the men returned to Earth they left 'foot prints on the Moon', not on most of the Moon but an equivalent to a football pitch and that Neil was the first to set foot on the surface of the Moon followed by Buzz.

It is circulated that Neil and Buzz have had Holy Communion in space or after the landing on the Moon and that when Neil visited the Holy Land (Israel) stated that walking in the footsteps of Jesus was more enjoyable than walking on the Moon. Also is circulated that Neil requested for no rescue mission should the landing fail. Neil died in 2012.

Mother Teresa
1910–1997

Mother Teresa was born in 1910 into an Albanian Catholic family in Skopje the current capital of Northern Republic of Macedonia but in pre-war 1914–18 was part of Kosovo ruled by the Turks and baptised the following day. Later, she became a Catholic nun.

She founded the order of the Missionaries of Charity which is run by women only helping the poor worldwide and especially in India which began in the 1950s. She said I see Jesus in the face of every human. Mother Teresa's work was highly recognised by both Church and secular circles. And when asked about her work which is so small compared to the ocean of needy and deprived humanity, she answered that the ocean is also made from drops.

She was awarded the secular Nobel Peace Prize in 1979 and described by secular media at the time 'diminutive' Catholic nun. Also was awarded the dual Indian nationality as a merit and recognition for her work among the poor and sick of India.

She was beatified in October 2003 (blessed) and Canonised in September 2016 as Saint Teresa of Calcutta (Kolkata in Indian)

Mother Teresa was a 'Pencil in God's hand' or as she said, 'I am a little pencil in God's hands.' Every human being who heard about her adored her, Christians and non-Christians, Catholics and non-Catholics. She died on 5 September 1997 and buried in Kolkata, India.

Arthur Blessitt
25 December 1969

On Christmas Day 1969 Arthur Blessitt started walking with his cross from Los Angeles to Washington D. C, then the world over.

He crossed many countries, islands and territories across the globe spanning 38102 miles carrying a wheeled 12-feet wooden cross and rested on his shoulder. His story is in his book titled:

'The Cross: 38102 Miles 38 Years 1 Mission.

Arthur Blessit is an American Evangelist and Missionary and contributor to Trinity Broadcasting Network TBN TV Channel founded in America by late Paul Crouch and is the largest Christian channel branched worldwide into 30 sub-channels to cater for 'heart-languages' other than English.

In the Gospel of Luke, only among the four Gospels, Jesus says in his own mother tongue in the classical Aramaic the lingua franca at the time 'If anyone would come after me, he must deny himself take up his cross daily and follow me' (Luke 9:23). The Polish poet Cyprian Norwid Quoted the Biblical verse 'Not with the Cross of the Saviour behind you, but with your own cross behind the Saviour.

This must have been said while Jesus walked down the alleyways of Jerusalem known now by the name Via Dolerosa carrying his heavy cross after the elite of his time sentenced him to die on the Mount of Calvary.

Arthur Blessitt was one of those to follow Jesus on Christmas Day 25 December 1969 and continued until 17 May 2008. That famed cross, one cross, three nails, five wounds and one Saviour.

Cardinal Joseph Ratzinger becomes Pope Benedict XVI 2005–2013

When Bishop of Rome Pope John Paul II (Polish national) died in 2005 Cardinal Joseph Ratzinger (German national) was elected a Pope on 19 April 2005 after 2-day conclave taking the name Benedict XVI.

Born in Bavaria on Holy Saturday and baptised on the same day in 1927, he and his brother entered the Catholic priesthood. He excelled among his colleagues and was destined for higher clerical office.

In 1977, he became the Archbishop of Munich and was promoted to cardinal the same year.

Cardinal Joseph Ratzinger was appointed as the head of the Congregation for the Doctrine of the Faith in 1981, a prestigious office in the Vatican administration and his election for papacy was almost certain.

In the Vatican circle there is a gossip that during the conclave a Cardinal who enters the conclave as a Pope leaves it as a cardinal, but Ratzinger entered as a cardinal and left it as a Pope.

Benedict XVI was a traditional Pope in the likes of John Paul I, Paul VI, John XXIII and Pius XII, unlike his predecessor or his successor in that they are more liberal-minded and statesmen-like. Benedict XVI is 'my type of guy'.

Pope Benedict XVI authored many books one of which I have is titled 'Jesus of Nazareth' and wrote it while in office as a Pope. He is a deep theologian in Christian faith.

During his papacy, unlike his predecessor or successor he was described by media as 'worried' about changing Europe and the direction Europe and the West were heading, something visibly clear at the time of his papacy. The decline was slow but sure.

Pope Benedict XVI introduced changes in the liturgy of the Catholic Mass among other things.

As a Pope he is the head of the Catholic Church and head of the Vatican City State which is a non-member observer of the UN General Assembly.

The Catholic Church is the greatest institution in the world with 0.5-1.0 million clerical, semi-clerical and nun personnel. The Catholic Church is 'the long running institution in the history of mankind' one observed.

The Catholic Church is 1.2 billion believers worldwide and Christianity as a whole is about 2.2 billion believers, just less than a third of humanity. Most densely Catholic countries are Brazil, Mexico, the Philippines, USA and Italy.

The Catholic Church sticks to its traditional and conservative teaching of the Gospel without dilution. It also teaches the infallibility of the Pope which means that the Pope cannot err in matters of faith but may err in personal matters.

Pope Benedict XVI retired in 2013, the first Pope to retire and was succeeded by Pope Francis.

Notre Dame Cathedral
15 April 2019

The Cathedral of Notre-Dame de Paris or Cathedral of Our Lady of Paris one of the world most famous Cathedrals was built on the site of an old church in an island created by the River Seine and dedicated to the Blessed Virgin Mary mother of Jesus. The Catholic Church and Christianity in general had just finished celebrating the 850 years anniversary of its foundation cornerstone in 2013.

But in the early evening and shortly after 6 PM local time on Monday 15 April 2019 a fire engulfed the building above the spire and spread throughout as shocked Christians and tourists watched in sorrow and disbelief.

Early work began in 1160 under King Louis VII and Pope Alexander III laid the foundation cornerstone in 1163 and the Cathedral was nearly completed in 1345.

The Cathedral went through many restorations and survived the upheaval of the French Revolution which was triggered on 14 July 1789 when the revolutionaries stormed the Bastille and survived the Nazi blitz of 1939–1945.

The shrine has the capacity of 3000 and contains relics and statues of Biblical kings. The relics, like fragment of the crown of thorn worn by Jesus during His crucifixion, nail from the Crucifixion cross and fragments of the wooden crucifixion cross are also preserved. The Cathedral attracts 12 million pilgrims and visitors annually.

In 1801, Napoleon Bonaparte returned the building to the Catholic Church and used the Cathedral for his coronation in 1804 and later his marriage to Marie-Louise of Austria in 1810.

The French writer Victor Hugo inspired by the Cathedral wrote his novel *The Hunchback of Notre Dame* after the revolution in 1831.

There was uproar of empathy from world leaders including President Donald Trump, and Mike Pence his Vice President who stated, 'It is heartbreaking to see a house of God in flames.' The incumbent French President said, 'Our Lady of Paris in flames.'

Although darkened by age it is one of the buzz centres for faithful and tourists.

'The triumph of the cross'

The triumph of the cross is a feast day in the Catholic Church and falls on 14 September each year. In the Middle East the feast is celebrated on the eve of that day with bonfires, fireworks and illuminations. The Orthodox Church also celebrates the feast. The cross has triumphed and will always triumph.

After the tragic and terror events of 11/9 2001 carried by 19 terrorists on four landmark political and economic targets, there stood a high metal cross from the remaining metal structure of collapsed buildings at Ground Zero in New York. It is the Cross of Jesus to remind us and the world that Jesus is here and with us and has not abandoned us.

On 12 January 2010 Haiti was hit by a powerful earthquake measured 7.0 on Richter scale equivalent to 0.5 million ton of TNT. The Caribbean nation of Haiti (9 millions) the poorest country in the western hemisphere suffered 230,000 dead, 300,000 injured and made 1.5 million displaced. Buildings, churches and infra structure collapsed but there among the ruins stood a huge crucifix of Jesus-Jesus nailed to the cross reminding us he is suffering with us and that he is with us.

In the Rome's Coliseum is a semi standing dark and archaic theatre where the Romans entertained themselves watching Christians being punished or devoured for their faith in Jesus Christ. Near the seat of Nero in the theatre there is a cross erected to remind the Romans that the cross triumphed over Nero when the whole Roman Empire accepted Jesus Christ in 313 AD. That event shifted the centre of gravity of Christendom to Rome.

Homily

In my first book titled *I am a Christian*, I explained what it means to be a Christian and is that to follow Jesus Christ and to believe in his birth, crucifixion, death, resurrection and his second coming.

I define Christianity as faith born in Bethlehem and via Galilee completes in Jerusalem. This means the 'virgin birth', preaching the Greek Gospel and the 'empty tomb'.

It is said that a person is innocent until proven guilty, but I say and in accordance with my Christian faith that a person is born guilty until proven innocent. This means Adam's guilt is in us and we cannot reach heaven without climbing the ladder through Jesus Christ. In Christ's sacrifice alone we are redeemed, there is no other redeemer.

I believe in the Hebrew Bible that 'God created the heavens and the earth' and in secular term means 'space-time-matter-energy'. God created nature, He created man and woman. God did not create anti-nature. Anti-nature was invented by man.

In the Hebrew Bible God says, 'Thou shall not kill,' which means do not play with nature, do not abort, and do not euthanize because life is sacred. The Catholic Church teaches that contraception is sin, because you prevent life and play with nature. The Christian church abhors abortion clinics and euthanasia clinics. The church is for life not death.

Jesus said while walking the alleyways of Via Dolorosa on that historical Friday with a heavy 'old rugged cross' on his shoulders – Deny, Carry and Follow. I will deny, I will carry, and I will follow.

In maths one plus one equals two but Jesus said is three, which means when I and you meet in His name Jesus will be the third among us.

Christian Stories

'Live Truth, live Catholic' is the slogan and motto of the Catholic television channel EWTN and I would like to paraphrase it into Live Truth, live Christian because the first is part of the latter.

I have heard these Christian stories in past years and all convey the Christian message of salvation through Jesus Christ only and the truth of his Gospel:

Mathematical Gospel

Parents and their child were watching Christian television channel when parents told the child to continue watching while they spend time in the garden.

Then a preacher appeared and started talking about maths in the gospel. He started by writing on the board $1+1+1=1$ and said the Father and the Son and the Holy Spirit are one Triune God.

Then he wrote on the board $1+1=1$ and said for this reason a man shall leave his father and mother and be united with his wife and be one.

Then he wrote on the board $1+1=3$ and said Jesus said if two are gathered in my name I will be the third among them.

Then he wrote on the board 100-1=100 and said the shepherd who lost one sheep left the 99 and went looking for the lost one and found it then reunited with 99 sheep to become 100.

At this time the parents joined their child and told them this preacher is a good preacher but all his maths is wrong.

(Based on 2Corinthians 13:14; Ephesians 5:31;Matthew 18:20; Luke 15:3-7).

I will wait for Jesus

A man fell into a ditch and he could not get out by himself. Charles passed by and wanted to help him but he could not. Karl passed by and he could not help. Sigmund passed he too could not help.

Then all past and present theorists and founders of religion passed by but they too could not help. Now all stood together and told the man if you climb half way we all could grab you out but the poor man could not do it.

Before it is too long the poor man said to them go all of you because you cannot do anything for me and I will wait for Jesus to come. All the men were angered and said if we all cannot do anything what would Jesus do?

He told them this is the second time I have fallen into this ditch. The first time Jesus passed by he looked at me and smiled. He came down to me, he hugged me, held me with his hand and we went up together.

Crossing the Red Sea

Two university students shared a flat together, one Christian the other not. When the Christian student read the Bible loud and saw a miracle of God he would shout Hallelujah Praise the Lord. Once reading the Book of Exodus and reaching to the point where the Red Sea parted and the Israelites crossed over he shouted Hallelujah Praise the Lord. His friend told what is it? He said the Red Sea parted and the Israelites crossed. His friend told him it was only a few inches of water.

The Christian student continued reading and reached the point when the Egyptian army followed them then the water rushed back drowning the Egyptian army. He shouted Hallelujah Praise the Lord. His friend told him what is it this time? He told him now the Egyptian army followed the Israelites and the water rushed back drowning all of them. His friend said how that can be? The Christian told him with those few inches of water.

Jonah in heaven

A young student at secondary school deep in Christian faith has to argue with his atheist teacher about the Bible. The teacher told him how do you believe in virgin birth and resurrection of Jesus? The student said it is in the Bible and I by faith believe that.

Then the teacher asked the student do you believe that Jonah was in the belly of a fish for three days and three nights? The student said yes I believe and I prove it to you when I die I will go to heaven and I will see Jonah and will ask him face to face. The teacher told the student suppose Jonah is in hell not heaven. The student said it is simple when you die and go to hell you ask him.

Daily bread

A Christian lady prayed daily and loudly many times a day the Lord's Prayer 'Our Father who art in heaven hallowed be thy name…give us this day our daily bread…' Her neighbour an atheist man was annoyed by her prayer. And one day he decided to stop her praying by going to supermarket and putting a pile of bread on the threshold of her door. The lady opens the door and finds plenty of bread at the front door. She rejoices and praises God but continued to pray.

Her neighbour got tired of this so he knocked on the door and the lady opened and told her that he was the one who put the bread at the threshold. It was from me and not from God.

The lady told him I prayed to God to give me bread and God can use anyone, you and even the devil to answer prayers. She told him I prayed to God to give me bread. God answered my prayer and gave me bread.

Jewish woman and her son

In Jewish tradition when a son or daughter or any relative leaves the Jewish faith, the family goes through a traditional 'wake' to lament the departure from the faith.

A devout Jewish lady went to her Rabbi sobbing that her son became a Christian. The Rabbi comforted her and told her that his own son also became Christian. He told her to go to the chief Rabbi.

She went to the chief Rabbi and told him that her son became a Christian. The chief Rabbi comforted her and told her his own son became a Christian. He told her go home and pray to God.

In the evening before going to bed she prayed and that night she had a dream and in it God said loud, 'My Son is a Christian.'

Marxism advocate and a preacher

In Marxist era in Eastern Europe a Marxist advocate was proclaiming the utopia of Marxism for every human being. He added Marxism will put a new suit on every man.

A devout Christian faithful was offended and started street preaching saying that the salvation of man is through Jesus Christ and that Jesus will put a new man in every suit.

A day equals a thousand years

A monk in a monastery in the desert had problem digesting what Saint Peter says in 2 Peter 3:8, that '…a day is like a thousand years, and a thousand years are like a day…'

He went to bed that evening troubled for failing to understand the meaning of the verse. In his dream while standing outside the monastery he saw a beautiful bird close to him, and he stretched his hands to touch it but the bird flew farther from him. He chased the bird within grasp of touching it but the bird gain escaped him and the saga goes on for a long distance and each time the bird evades the monk, until they reached the nearest town.

The monk was shocked to see the town, its buildings, people and culture in a more advanced way. He asked some people how the town was and how it is now. They told him it was a thousand years ago. His alarm clock rings and he wakes and said to himself – my Lord and my God – Eureka!

The Christian Faith in Quotations

In my first book titled *I am a Christian*, I have listed some good number of Christian quotes but in this book I will go for more. The purpose of these quotations is that if you sum up all these quotes you will have the full picture of the Christian faith and the truth of our Saviour Jesus Christ. If you are a Christian that is fine, become more Christian but, if you are not, hurry up and follow Jesus. The quotes are in ad hoc order.

'…I am who I am…' – God (Exodus 3:14)

'…before Abraham was born, I am!' – Jesus Christ (John 8:58)

'…Let my people go…' – Moses (Exodus 9:1)

'From the chirping of the birds, the mooing of the cows, the voices and tumult of human beings from all of these one hears the voice, the unceasing voice, of God in the Torah.' – Kalonymus Kalman Shapira, 1889–1943.

'Man is made in the image and likeness of God, and that Jesus Christ is the image of that invisible God.' – Benjamin Harnwell.

'Christianity is not about changing lives. It is about exchanging lives.' – Anonymous

'The Law was good, New Testament is better.' – Anonymous

'Jesus is not 2000 years memory. He is here with us.' – Anonymous

'Christmas simply would not exist as we know it without Jesus.' – Anonymous

'Jesus is the Bible, the walking Bible.' – Anonymous

'Christianity is a global religion…' – Anonymous

'If you don't live the Gospel, how can you preach the Gospel?' – Anonymous

'Jesus came into the world precisely to offer us a return to Eden, if we follow him.' – Anonymous

'…if you are feeling far away from God, it is not God who moved…' – Anonymous

'We believe in rationality. We believe in reason. We believe in science. We believe in the existence of God.' – RDOF.ORG

'The Civilisation of Love is the Way of the Church.' – Anonymous

'The Bible is not an ordinary book it is the Word of God.' – Anonymous

'If you want to walk on water, you have to step out of the boat.' – Anonymous

'Noah was saved from the waters while we as Saint Peter points out are saved by the waters of Baptism.' – Anonymous

'This [New] Covenant will see God and Man living more closely together.' – Anonymous

'Have a Hallelujah not a Halloween.' – Anonymous
'Jesus has many fans but few disciples.' – Anonymous

'Christ is our silent friend who is always there…' – Anonymous

'There are no gray areas with God.' – Anonymous

'…but the last and greatest salvation brought by Jesus is harder to understand: saved from sin and death.' – Anonymous

'…you are spirit, you have a soul, and you live in a body.' – Jonathan Oloyede
'No one knows what the future holds, except the One who holds the future.' – Eric Metaxas

'Christians recognize that our planet was uniquely designed and fined-tuned to support life-and that's putting it mildly. Our place in the universe is nothing less than a miracle.' – Eric Metaxas

'If you want to help the Jewish people to build our homeland, the Bible Land here in Judea and Samaria, you must vote for Donald Trump, a real friend of the State of Israel.' – Yossi Dagan

'Jesus is the only answer for the world.' – Ward Simpson

'…He is the beginning and the end. He is the Commander of the Armies of God. He is the Way, the Truth, and the Life. He is the One who holds the power of life and death. He has already won the battle and He has already prepared a place for us. He is our soon and coming King, the Lord Jesus Christ!' – Ward Simpson

'…let's continue to penetrate the darkness over the earth with the good news of Jesus Christ.' – Ward Simpson

'Jesus Christ, the light of the world, The Way, The Truth and The Life. Jesus Christ, the answer for the world, yesterday, today and forever more.' – Ward Simpson

'The mission is the Gospel, the method is media. God TV broadcasting the good news of Jesus Christ to the nations of the world.' – Ward Simpson

'…Salvation is not a system, it is not a formula, it is not even a prayer. Salvation is a person. His name is Jesus/Yeshua which means salvation.' – Ward Simpson

'Blessed is he who expecteth nothing, for he shall enjoy everything.' – Dale Ahlquist

'Jesus Christ is your champion.' – David Borg

'Jesus is the door; there is no other door, there is not a side door. There is not another name under heaven and earth; Jesus and Jesus only, the only way.' – Sandra Kennedy

'Heaven has no expiration date, it is eternal…heaven is forever.' – Sandra Kennedy

'The most important event in human history is the virgin birth, because without the virgin birth, there is no Calvary and there is no Resurrection.' – Sandra Kennedy

'…is he the son of Mary or the Son of God? He's both.' – David Jeremiah

'Jesus was the first missionary.' – David Jeremiah

'If there is no Christmas, we cannot know God.' – David Jeremiah

'If there is no Christmas, we cannot be forgiven.' – David Jeremiah

'If there is no Christmas, we cannot be understood.' – David Jeremiah

'If there is no Christmas, we cannot have hope.' – David Jeremiah

'I am neither a prophet nor the son of a prophet even though I have a prophet name.' – David Jeremiah

'The greatest gift God gave to the world is Jesus Christ but the greatest gift Jesus Christ gave to the church is the Holy Spirit and the greatest gift the Holy Spirit has given to every believer is the ability to speak the Holy Language (speaking in tongues).' – Fire Conference

'It is better to vote for a good Protestant than for a bad Catholic.' – Cardinal Muller

'Come, Lord Jesus Maranatha. Come, Lord Jesus Maranatha.' – Timothy Michael Dolan

'Death is not a chance for some of us, but a certainty for all of us.' – William Philip

'I would rather stand with God and be judged by the world, than stand with the world and be judged by God.' – Grace Wesley

'This is not an age in which to be a soft Christian.' – Francis Schaeffer

'Reformation is a return to the sound doctrine of the Bible. Revival is the practice of that sound doctrine under the power of the Holy Spirit.' – Francis Schaeffer

'To be always united with Jesus, this is my life program.' – Carlo Acutis, 1991–2006

'I am happy to die because I have lived my life without wasting a minute on those things that do not please God.' – Carlo Acutis, 1991–2006

'Your legal career is but a means to an end and…that end is building the Kingdom of God.' – Amy Coney Barratt

'The Bible will keep you from sin, or sin will keep you from the Bible.' – Dwight Lyman Moody, 1837–1899

'The worst of days with Jesus are still better than the best of days without him.' – Misty Edwards

'Christian life isn't a one-person race. It's a relay…' – Christine Caine

'Jesus didn't come to make us safe. He came to make us dangerous to the kingdom of darkness.' – Christine Caine

'Don't allow your history to define your destiny.' – Christine Caine

'Where governments tried to kill God, they have often turned next to killing people.' EWTN Catholic TV channel

'Without morals, a republic cannot subsist any length of time; they therefore who are decrying the Christian religion…are undermining the solid foundation of morals, the best security for the duration of free governments.' – Charles Carroll 1737–1832

'In Christ Jesus there is an overflow of victory.' – Bob Cornell

'I am a yes man to the Word of God.' – Bob Cornell

'Wherever he went Paul preached Jesus.' – Bob Cornell

'The church needs to come back to Calvary.' – Bob Cornell

'There is no class system in the cross.' – Bob Cornell

'Be Biblically correct-not politically correct.' – Michael Youssef

'When you do the possible, God will do the impossible.' – Michael Youssef

'As goes the pulpit, so goes the pew. As goes the pew, so goes the nation.' – Michael Youssef

'Pope John Paul II and Ronald Reagan were a match made in heaven.' – Paul Kengor

'Ronald Reagan and John Paul II would partner together for a great victory: the defeat of atheistic Soviet communism.'
– Paul Kengor

'Christianity is the least complex and the most inclusive of any religion in the world.' – Robert Morris

'We are born selfish, we are born again generous.' – Robert Morris

'I am more excited stepping on these stones [Jesus' footsteps] than I was stepping on the Moon.' – Neil Armstrong, 1930–2012

'Great moves of God are usually preceded by simple acts of obedience.' – Steve Furtick

'Your identity is not in what you posses, but who posses you.' – Creflo Dollar

'When you come to religion, you come to a place. When you come to Jesus Christ, you come to a person.' – Ravi Zacharias 1946–2020

'The world was made for the body. The body was made for the soul. And the soul was made for God.' – Ravi Zacharias 1946–2020

'God trained Moses in a palace to use him in a desert. He trained Joseph in a desert to use him in a palace.' – Ravi Zacharias 1946-2020

'The cross is the Gospel. Without the cross there is no Gospel.' – Bill Bailey

'Jesus is the source. The cross is the means.' – Bill Bailey

'The hinge of history can be found on a Bethlehem door.' – J. John

'The Pope is not a theological dictator.' Mitch Pacwa

'The Mass is about Jesus Christ, not us.' Mitch Pacwa

'The Church has no authority to change [the Bible].' – Charles Pope

'…We are here to follow Jesus Christ, to bear witness to His love in our lives, and to build His Kingdom on earth.' – Jose Gomez

'We are not sinners because we sin. We sin because we are sinners.' – R. C. Sproul

'God is everywhere, even in the news.' – CBN

'[Donald Trump] an immovable friend of Israel.' – George Pompeo

'Israel is mentioned in the Bible 2000 times.' – God TV

'God created women with special role, to reveal facets of His character and His love in a unique way.' – TBN

'It is good to take time out with God, have a stress-free moment or two, and renew our minds with God's Word.' – TBN

'In China one million people come to [Christian] faith every year.' – Bible Society

'…one Nation under God, indivisible, with liberty and justice for all…' – The Pledge of Allegiance to the Flag 1954

'Christianity is not a sprint but an endurance run.' – John Bevere

'The Cross will not crush you; if its weight makes you stagger, its power will also sustain you.' – Saint Padre Pio, 1887–1968

'The habit of asking "Why" has ruined the world.' – Saint Padre Pio, 1887–1968

'The message of Passover remains as powerful as ever. Freedom is won not on the battlefield but in the classroom and the home…' – Jonathan Sacks, 1948–2020

'You do not realise that it is better for you that one man die for the people than that the whole nation perish.' – Joseph Caiaphas (John 11:50)

'May the Christ-child of Bethlehem find in your heart the manger for which He longs.' – Michael Quinlan

'God has been with us all along-He is not fazed by Covid-19.' – Richard Fleming

'A humanism which excludes God is an inhuman humanism.' – Benedict XVI

'The world offers you comfort. But you were not made for comfort. You were made for greatness.' – Benedict XVI

'[Year] 2021 offers the opportunity to look with fresh eyes towards Yeshua (Jesus)-the pioneer and perfecter of our faith.' – Ron Cantor

'Israel isn't just a place that God was. It's a place where God is…' – Kirt Schneider

'I am not a singer. I am a praiser.' – Kirt Schneider

'There is always death at the end of your plan and life at the end of God's plan…' – Rod Parsley

'As world events develop, prophecy becomes more and more exciting…' – Hal Lindsey

'A day will come when the civilized world will deny its God, when the Church will doubt…' – Pius XII 1876-1958

'Through some crack the smoke of Satan has entered into the Church of God.' – Paul VI, 1897–1978

'We are not the sum of our weaknesses and failures; we are the sum of the Father's love for us and our real capacity to become the image of his Son.' – John Paul II, 1920–2005

'…War is not always inevitable. It is always a defeat for humanity.' – John Paul II 1920–2005

'It was Christ who willingly went to the cross, and it was our sins that took him there.' – Franklin Graham

'God's word is the same, yesterday and today and a million years from now.' – Franklin Graham

'My father [Billy Graham] preached on heaven, told millions how to find heaven, he wrote a book on heaven and today he is in heaven.' – Franklin Graham

'Radical Christianity is not going on a mission's trip or a big conference. Radical Christianity is staying steady for decades.' – Mike Bickle

'We had 10,337 people in the seats last Sunday…because I get things done.' – Keith Butler

'Dedication is writing your name on the bottom of a blank sheet of paper and handling it to the Lord for Him to fill in…' – Rick Renner

'God is never too late, nor too early, but just on time.' – R. T. Kendall

'There is superficial conflict but deeper concord between science and theistic religion, but superficial concord and deep conflict between science and naturalism.' – Alvin Plantinga

'…God does not reward us based on how many people we lead to Jesus. He rewards based on our obedience and faithfulness to His call and will.' – Daniel Kolenda

'I was kidnapped…but refused to renounce Christ.' – Amina

'Are you a follower of Christ or just an admirer of Christ?' – Thomas John Joseph Paprocki

'God had one son on earth without sin, but never one without suffering.' – Saint Augustine of Hippo 354-430

'The men who have done the most for God in this world have been early on their knees…' E. M. Bounds

'First of all, the power is in the gospel…' – Michael Brown

'The New Testament is more like looking at the bigger picture…' – Michael Brown

'I think at the heart of the pro-life movement is the idea that all people are created equal, endowed by their creator with certain unalienable rights starting with life.' – Mike Huckabee

'Before we can pray, "Lord, Thy Kingdom come", we must be willing to pray, "My Kingdom go"...' – Alan Redpath

'Jesus did not come to make God's love possible, but to make God's love visible.' – Daystar

'We cannot live without Sunday.' – Martyrs of Abitene

'...our God is the God of yesterday, today and tomorrow.' – Al Jandl

'Christmas is about [Immanuel's] Presence, not Presents.' – Mary-Rose Verret

'The Teacher is more than the Teaching.' – Scot Mcknight

'I have "the God Code.' – T. D. Jakes

We are all sinners in need of a Saviour.' – Billy Wilson

'I realize on that cross the body of our Lord is bearing the sin and the weight of guilt for all mankind for all of time.' – Billy Wilson

'The cross is a spiritual force.' – Billy Wilson

'The cross was a global event.' – Billy Wilson

'...this Jesus, not the historical Jesus. He is here and now.' – Guillermo Maldonado

'Your faith is more precious than your job.' – Guillermo Maldonado

'My faith is bigger than cancer.' – Guillermo Maldonado

'We have a message of Good News to proclaim just as much today as we ever have done!' – Bob Chambers

'There is power in prayer. When men work, they work, but when men pray, God works.' – Angus Buchan

'We cannot keep the Good News to ourselves any longer! Time is running out.' – Angus Buchan

'There is no grey area in the Bible…' – Angus Buchan

'Attempt great things for God and expect great things from God.' – William Carey

'…God's plans are not thwarted by our trials, rather the gospel goes out.' – Ramzi Adcock

'The message of Jesus Christ is a message for everyone.' – Bobby Houston

'The Sabbath [Saturday or Sunday] is a window to eternity.' – Joseph Mary

'Temptation is a lie.' – Joseph Mary

'I saw many, many Christians killed without reason just because they're Christians.' – Michaeel Najeeb

'God will use whatever he wants to display his glory. Heavens and stars. History and nations. People and problems.' – Max Lucado

'God turned my life upside down…' – Kate Nicholas

'…Our mission is to create a church so large, that it transforms society one person at a time-demonstrating our extraordinary God!' – Sophia Barrett

'We were never designed to receive glory. We were designed to give glory.' – Darlene Zschech

'The presence of God makes a difference between heaven and hell.' – Derek Walker

'We stand with Israel. We stand with Israel. We stand with Israel.' – Donnie Swaggart

'God is greater than your sin.' – Donnie Swaggart

'Jesus in the morning, Jesus in the afternoon, Jesus in the evening…' – Loren Larson

'Jesus even kept the Sabbath in death.' – Loren Larson

'Someday you will read in the papers that D. L. Moody of East Northfield is dead. Don't you believe a ward of it! At that moment I shall be more alive than I am now. I shall have gone up higher that is all, out of this old clay tenement into a house that is immortal-a body that death cannot touch, that sin cannot taint; a body fashioned like unto His glorious body.' – Dwight L. Moody, 1837–1899

'I was born of the flesh in 1837. I was born of the Spirit in 1856. That which is born of the flesh may die. That which is born of the Spirit will live forever.' – Dwight L. Moody, 1837–1899

'If I was to meet those slave raiders that abducted me and those who tortured me, I'd kneel down to them to kiss their hands, because if it had not have been for them, I would not have become a Christian and a religious woman.' Saint Josephine Bakhita, 1869–1947

'Richard [Bewes] was a man who carried a Bible in his pocket and Jesus in his heart.' – Michael Baughen

'Our gains are almost all external, and our losses are wholly internal.' – Aiden Wilson Tozer 1897-1963

'Everybody worships. Whether Christian or atheist…' – Matt Redman

'We have really lost in our society the sense of the sacredness of life.' – Basil Hume, 1923–1999

'I come without five lire. I want to leave without five lire.' – John Paul I, 1912–1978

'God is our father, but even more is God our mother.' – John Paul I, 1912–1978

'God moves in power, in signs and wonders…' – Randy Clark

'For many Charismatic, Scripture is not simply a book to be read and studied but it is an invitation into a lifestyle of supernatural engagement…' – Randy Clark

'The fear of God illumines the soul, annihilates evil, weakens the passions, drives darkness from the soul and makes it pure…' – Saint Aphrem of Edessa, 306–373

'If thou wouldst rule well, thou must rule for God, and to do that thou must be ruled by him…Those who will not be governed by God will be ruled by tyrants.' – William Penn, 1644–1718

'It is time for the church to stop flirting with the world.' – Alan Scotland

'The Bible carries the Word of God.' – Alan Scotland

'We know the end from the beginning.' – Alan Scotland

'I am so glad Jesus came into my life.' – Alan Scotland

'Jesus is everything.' – Tommy Lilja

'I am leaving the boat in the name of Jesus.' – Tommy Lilja

'The Salvation Army: A force for good in today's world.'
– The Salvation Army

'Inspired by our Christian faith, The Salvation Army works to serve helping suffering humanity…' – The Salvation Army

'The Salvation Army is often called Christianity with its sleeves rolled up.' – Dean Pallant

'We who have Christ's eternal life need to throw away our own lives.' – George Verwer

'The message of the Gospel is one of transformation, and millions have experienced its power in their life and community, through their encounter with one of our [OM] ships.' – Seelan Govender

'Everyone who is redeemed is saved by faith in the sacrifice of Jesus. All the saints from Adam to John the Baptist were saved by looking forward in faith to the cross…' – Doug Batchelor

'Christianity doesn't offer a smooth flight; it promises a safe landing. The promise of Jesus is not one of happiness, He promises righteousness.' – Ray Comfort

'Darwinian evolution is unscientific, unobservable, unbelievable, but understandable in a world that hates God.' – Ray Comfort

'God created us to be dependent on him.' – Andrew Wommack

'Without faith, God's grace is wasted and without grace, faith is powerless.' – Andrew Wommack

'Remember this you cannot change the laws of God.' – Richard Stanley

'God will never reject you. Whether you accept Him is your decision.' – Charles Stanley

'The time you spend alone with God will transform your character and increase your devotion…' – Charles Stanley

'I'm eradicating the word Protestant even out of my vocabulary…I'm protesting anything…it's time for Catholics and non-Catholics to come together as one in the Spirit and one in the Lord.' – Paul Crouch, 1934–2013

'Ours is an age that's often obsessed with knowledge at the expense of wisdom.' – Mal Fletcher

'…You have the cure [Jesus] to death…go out there and share it.' – Kirk Cameron

'I 'm not perfect in my walk but I want to do the right thing.' – Kirk Cameron

'Oh beloved, no matter the intensity of the furnace you may find yourself in, our beloved Heavenly Father is goodness…oh, so full of grace.' – Wendy Alec

'I have nothing to hide. I am a servant of the living God. He is the only one I answer to.' – Benny Hinn

'He who has Christ has all he needs and needs no more.' – Jonathan Edwards, 1703–1758

'Nature is God's greatest evangelist.' – Jonathan Edwards, 1703–1758

'Truth is the agreement of our ideas with the ideas of God.' – Jonathan Edwards, 1703–1758

'Every Christian family ought to be as it were a little church.' – Jonathan Edwards, 1703–1758

'You contribute nothing to your salvation except the sin that made it necessary.' – Jonathan Edwards, 1703–1758

'God doesn't come to kill, to steal, or to destroy. That's the enemy. God comes to give abundant life. Know your God so you don't get confused.' – Mike Pilavachi

'Prayer is a weapon…' – Peter Forsyth, 1848–1921

'The mega-strategy of Jesus, make disciples.' – David Platt

'Jesus loves you, loves you, loves you, no matter who you are.' – V. Dilkumar

'I always say, I have a cure for the malignancy of the soul. And he has name and it's Jesus…' – Kathie Lee Gifford

'The Good News, the Doctor is in, He conquered death for all-time for every one of us and it's free…' – Kathie Lee Gifford

'The laws of God, like the law of gravity, do not depend upon how I feel about them. They are inexorable.' – Scot Hahn

'Luke: The Gospel of the Saviour for Lost People Everywhere.' – Mark L. Strauss

'God loves you because of whom you are but he blesses you because of what you do.' – Mike Murdock

'What you make happen for others, God will make happen for you.' – Mike Murdock

'Going to church doesn't make a Christian.' – Bill Sunday, 1862–1935

'Worship is like breathing: You're created to do it all the time. It's a lifestyle.' – Joseph L. Garlington

'Jesus is the lion of the tribe of Judah.' – John Francis

'Peace is more powerful than war.' – Francis

'Terrorism and death never have the last word.' – Francis

'It is [Lent] the right time to turn off the television and open the Bible. It is the time to disconnect from cell phones and connect ourselves to the Gospel.' – Francis

'A soul that trusts God is invincible.' – Mother Mary Angelica, 1923–2016

'We are all called to be great saints, don't miss the opportunity.' – Mother Mary Angelica 1923-2016

'Remember, vote for life. It may be your own!' – Mother Mary Angelica, 1923–2016

'If you're not a thorn in somebody's side you aren't doing Christianity right.' – Mother Mary Angelica, 1923–2016

'While I'm waiting, I'm getting stronger, my faith is rising, and I will run on.' – Travis Greene

'The Creator comes to his creation [earth].' – John Ankerberg

'God is outside time and space because He created time and space…' – Joseph Prince

'God is righteous in making the sinner righteous.' – Joseph Prince

'The Law demands. Grace supplies.' – Joseph Prince

'Testing, Temptations, and Trials will become a Triumph when we trust God!' – Ed Young

'The Gospel of Jesus Christ, the Great Physician, heals people and makes them whole again...' – Ed Young

'Only Christianity and its teachings can explain the purpose and meaning of this world...' – Ken Ham

'It's time for a new Reformation in the Church...' – Ken Ham

'Prayer awards mighty victories. Prayer breaks down strongholds. Prayer is a mighty spiritual weapon...' – Ulf Ekman

'We must give up all that we are in order to possess all that He is.' – Heidi Baker

'Ministry is not about where you are or where you go, it is about where He is.' – Heidi Baker

'You are a paintbrush in the hands of the Artist.' – Heidi Baker

'Since nothing but God is eternal, nothing but God is worth the loving.' – Stephen Charnock, 1628–1680

'God, either you come down here tonight and touch me, or I'm going to die and come up there and touch you...' – Rodney Howard-Browne

'Peace and justice are two sides of the same coin.' – Dwight D. Eisenhower, 1890–1969

'…I would be standing before such a priest at the Easter Vigil Mass, publicly confessing my desire to be received into the largest, oldest male-helmed institution in the world, the Roman Catholic Church…' – Abigail Favale

'COVID-19. Unaccountable deaths in so many parts of the world. So much suffering and so many broken hearts. Who could have imagined such a long Good Friday? When are we going to see the Easter Sunday of COVID-19?' – Comboni Mission

'Easter is the biggest feast of Christianity, when we celebrate the victory of life over death.' – Comboni Mission

'…we do not live to die but die to live forever.' – Comboni Mission

'Bible is the wisdom bank.' – David Abiyeomie

'If you are born again you are born to reign.' – David Abiyeomie

'A Wordless Christian is a worthless Christian.' – David Abiyeomie

'I make myself a leper with the lepers to gain all to Jesus Christ.' – Saint Damien of Molokai 1840-1889

'God uses ordinary people to do extraordinary things.' – Jack Graham

'Temptation is not a sin.' – Jack Graham

'Jesus brought us back to the Garden [of Eden].' – Bill Winston

'…inside you is Christ, the Lion of the tribe of Judah.' – Bill Winston

'God is at work, let Him work through you.' – Rich Marshall

'Don't just praise God for what you can see, praise God for what you cannot see.' – Paul Adefarasin

'The love of Jesus is more than anything in the world.' – Rich Marshall

'Live for Jesus all the days of your life.' – Steven Brooks

'Our sins tower over our heads; they reach as high as the heavens.' 1 Esdras 8:75 GNB

'I begged you to be my people so that I could be your God…' – 2 Esdras 1:29 GNB

'A nation that turns away from prayer will ultimately find itself in desperate need of it.' – Jonathan Cahn

'As an atheist, I truly believe that Africa needs God.' – Justin Taylor

'When the devil reminds you of your past, remind him of his future!' – Saint Teresa of Avila, 1515–1582

'In the continuing shifting marketplace of ideas, religious concepts and speculations about our spiritual destiny, there is one book which stands apart from all other volumes ever written. That book is the Bible. The Bible claims not just to contain the Word of God but to be the Word of God. The religious fashions of men today often espouse a man-pleasing philosophy which claims that no one religion or faith has an exclusive right to claim to be "the truth". The desire of many religious people is to join in a great ecumenical world church in which each participant sheds his distinctive doctrine in the interests of religious harmony for the whole community of faiths. This process produces exactly what the participants' desire: a lowest common denominator of accepted generalities.' – Grant R. Jeffrey, 1948–2012

'The opposite of theism is not atheism it's idolatry!' – Kyle Idleman

'We love others best when we love God most.' – Kyle Idleman

'We are Easter people.' – Leo Patalinghug

'Our Church is a hospital for sinners.' – Leo Patalinghug

'The answer is to be found in the way in which we share in the triune splendor of the Good, the True and the Beautiful.'
– Joseph Pearce

'…So Mary's Son is the Sun; for she is the moon.' – Fulton J. Sheen 1895–1979

'Bye now and I love you.' – Fulton J. Sheen 1895–1979

'…It is finished…' – Jesus Christ (John 19:30)

Epilogue

My Christianity is Bible-based, Christ-cantered and not conquered by the world. Bible-based is a reference to every verse in the Bible in the Old and in the New Testaments. Christ-centred is reference that Jesus is the Son of God and the only way to the Father. Not-conquered by the world is a reference that the Bible is for all-time, all generations past, present and future, not a diluted or 'redefined' to align with the world or please the passer-bys.

I am able to expand in more details but want to avoid that believing that the three above statements of belief even though are concise they are very clear. That belief, made me suggest the title of this book, *My Christianity*.

Appendix
Psalm 137 NIV

"By the Rivers of Babylon we sat and wept
when we remembered Zion.

There on the poplars
we hung our harps,

for there our captors asked us for songs,
our tormentors demanded songs of joy;
they said, 'sing us one of the songs of Zion.'

How can we sing the songs of the LORD
while in a foreign land?

If I forget you, Jerusalem,
may my right hand forget its skill

May my tongue cling to the roof of my mouth
if I do not remember you,
if I do not consider Jerusalem
my highest joy.

Remember, LORD, what the Edomites did
on the day Jerusalem fell,
'Tear it down,' they cried,
'Tear it down to its foundations!'

Daughter Babylon, doomed to destruction,
happy is the one who repays you
according to what you have done to us.

Happy is the one who seizes your infants
and dashes them against the rocks."

By the Rivers of Babylon

The Melodians 1970

"By the rivers of Babylon
There we sat down
Ye-eah we wept
When we remembered Zion
By the rivers of Babylon
There we sat down
Ye-eah we wept
When we remembered Zion
When the wicked
Carried us away in captivity
Required from us a song
Now how shall we sing the Lord's song
In a strange land
When the wicked
Carried us away in captivity

Requiring of us a song
Now how shall we sing the Lord's song
In a strange land
Let the words of our mouth and
The meditations of our heart
Be acceptable in Thy sight here tonight
Let the words of our mouth and
The meditations of our heart
Be acceptable in Thy sight here tonight
By the rivers of Babylon
There we sat down
Ye-eah we wept
When we remembered Zion
By the rivers of Babylon
There we sat down
Ye-eah we wept
When we remembered Zion
By the rivers of Babylon
Dark tears of Babylon
There we sat down
You got to sing a song
Ye-eah we wept
Sing a song of love
When we remembered Zion
Yeah yeah yeah yeah yeah
By the rivers of Babylon
Rough bits of Babylon
There we sat down
You hear the people cry
Ye-eah we wept
Sing a song of love

When we remembered Zion
Yeah yeah yeah yeah yeah"

Confession

I am a Christian

I believe in God the Father
I believe in God the Son
I believe in God the Holy Spirit
I believe in the Bible, the whole Bible the Word of God
I believe in Virgin birth, Crucifixion, Resurrection and Ascension
I believe in Pentecost, the birth of the Church
I believe in church transformed not conformed
I believe in church that conquers not church conquered.

I am a Christian

I believe in Genesis one one
I believe in Genesis five two
I believe in Isaiah seven fourteen
I believe in John one one
I believe in John three three
I believe in John three sixteen
I believe in John fourteen six
I believe in John nineteen thirty

I believe in Matthew twenty-eight six
I believe in Acts two
I believe in Matthew twenty-eight nineteen
I believe in Revelation twenty-two seven

Prayer

Thank you Lord

"I was lost"
"Now am found"
I was "born once"
Now am "born twice"
I was "conformed"
Now I am "transformed"
I was dead
Now am alive
I was directionless
Now have directions
I was motionless
Now am in motion
I was condemned
Now am redeemed
I was voiceless
Now have a voice
I was worthless
Now am worth
I was unblessed
Now am blessed
I was disciple-less

Now am disciple-ed
I was wordless
Now am in the Word
I was fatherless
Now am in the Father
I was Christ-less
Now am in Christ
I was spiritless
Now am in Spirit
I was kingdom-less
Now am in the Kingdom

Thank you Lord
Amen.

'We are hard pressed on every side, but not crushed; perplexed but not in despair; persecuted, but not abandoned; struck down; but not destroyed.' 2 Corinthians 4:8-9

'For I am already being poured out like a drink offering, and the time has come for my departure. I have fought the good fight, I have finished the race, I have kept the faith.' 2 Timothy 4:6-7